for

much love

Cathy

The
MEANING
of LIFE

Compiled by
Jonathan Gabay

Dedicated to my wife and son
Without them I would have more questions than answers

As part of the International Red Cross and Red Crescent Movement, the British Red Cross Society (charity no. 220949) does not discriminate against race, colour or beliefs, either of its members and supporters or when providing humanitarian assistance to those who need help.

The Society would like to express its thanks to Jonathan Gabay, each contributor and Virgin Publishing for their generous support. However, the views expressed in this publication are those of the individual contributors and cannot be endorsed by the British Red Cross.

All royalties due to the author from this book have been donated to the British Red Cross, a registered charity.

First published in Great Britain in 1995 by
Virgin Books
an imprint of Virgin Publishing Ltd
332 Ladbroke Grove
London W10 5AH

A catalogue record for this book is available from the British Library

ISBN 1 85227 592 8

Typeset by SX Composing Ltd, Rayleigh, Essex
Printed and bound in Great Britain by
Butler & Tanner Ltd, Frome and London

CONTENTS

A PERSONAL MESSAGE FROM
HER MAJESTY QUEEN NOOR OF JORDAN

I am pleased to be associated with this book. The British Red Cross has always represented a shining example of compassion, dedication and courage.

By caring for people in crisis, the International Red Cross and Red Crescent Movement provides more than life-saving medical assistance delivered right to the heart of communities in need. Innocent victims whose lives are disrupted can all too easily lose their trust in their fellow man. Thanks to the Red Cross the anguish and suffering of so many around the world has been alleviated and their faith and hope restored.

His Majesty King Hussein and I, as co-Honorary Presidents of the Jordan National Red Crescent Society, have supported with pride and appreciation the commitment and dynamism of our own Red Crescent Society in its humanitarian activities in Jordan and the region, particularly in moments of crisis and disaster.

In 1995, to celebrate the 125th birthday of the British Red Cross, King Hussein and I were delighted to share in the celebration of your achievements over the past 125 years by opening a traditional street party for children in London's Oxford Street. As I looked upon their happy faces, I thought about the many children and their families throughout the world that have been helped by the British Red Cross. Outstanding doctors, nurses and volunteers reflect and convey the noblest attributes of the human spirit.

I have always been comforted by the wisdom of the Koran. The Prophet Muhammad teaches us that God looks upon men's hearts and deeds. As I look towards 1996, the 50th anniversary of the Hashemite Kingdom of Jordan and beyond, I think again of the children – my children, indeed, all children and their families, wherever they may be. We are each obliged to depend on one another for the future. As long as the world can continue to have faith in humanity's ability to care for and uphold the principles of life, we can be secure in our hopes for our children.

INTRODUCTION

Have you ever wondered what life is really all about? Some time ago I posed the 'big question' to people throughout the world. Not just academics, but a cross-section of people from dustmen to zoologists who I felt could offer a unique perspective on life today.

What follows are their answers. I thank every contributor who has cared enough to take the time to answer my question even if due to production restrictions I couldn't include them here. In addition to helping the life-saving work of the British Red Cross, their answers have given me encouragement, strength and insight.

Additionally I thank John Gray for his belief in this project as well as Robert Spigel and all the staff at the British Red Cross. Also Rod Green, Lorna Russell and the talented team at Virgin Publishing, Guy Facey of Amhurst Brown Colombotti Solicitors, Lesley Hadcroft and staff of Laurence Pollinger, and Copyright Promotions and its clients. And finally, my inspirational mother, courageous father and entire family.

Finding the meaning of life is an ongoing journey for everyone. Read this book like a map. It should help you to arrive at the destination of your choice. I sincerely hope that besides raising money for charity, this book provides you with comfort and happiness through greater understanding.

J. Jonathan Gabay

A

Life is a child playing around your feet, a tool you hold firmly in your grip, a bench you sit down upon in the evening, in your garden.
JANE ANOULTH

The acts of creatures are created and determined by God.
AL ASH'ARI

The purpose of man's life is not happiness, but worthiness.
FELIX ADLER

DANIELLE AARONS-MEGHAN

COCA-COLA NEW PRODUCT CATEGORY MANAGER (SOUTH PACIFIC)

Danielle was born in 1964. She graduated from Sydney University with a degree in business studies and marketing. She lives in Sydney, Australia, and at the time of writing this contribution was busy making preparations for her forthcoming marriage to a prominent British businessman.

Life, I imagine, is a little like the trip our family used to take to my grandmother's house.

She lived in the country, a four to five hour drive from our place.

There were two possible routes which we could take.

Via the main highway, a four hour drive, three minutes fifty if my father had the inclination (which was a rare occurrence indeed). My mother would further enhance the efficiency of this journey by waking us up at the crack of dawn, packing a thermos and sandwiches, and letting no one stop in our way.

My father preferred the 'alternative route'. Five hours of bumpy, winding road, some of it dirt, but oh the view . . . ocean, mountains, wildflowers.

He didn't think of the extra elbow grease needed to clean the car when we reached our destination, rather he thought of the family picnic we would have on the side of that bumpy road.

Life is a bumpy, winding road. We can all too easily place our feet on invisible accelerators going down endless highways – fast.

I myself, prefer the art of picnics and wildflower smelling.

LORD JEFFREY ARCHER

POLITICIAN AND NOVELIST

Lord Archer was born on 15 April 1940. His career has broadly been divided between writing and politics. As an author, his work has included Not a Penny More, Not a Penny Less, Kane and Abel *and* A Matter of Honour. *He has been a member of the GLC for Havering, a local MP and Deputy Chairman of the Conservative Party.*

Jeffrey Archer

6th May 1994

Dear Mr Gabay

Many thanks for your letter of 5th May.

I am not certain I know the meaning of life but I have two maxims -

1   "The heights by great men reached and kept
were not attained by sudden flight,
but they, while their companions slept,
were toiling upward in the night".

Henry Wadworth Longfellow 1807-1882.

2   Energy plus talent you're a King
Energy plus no talent you're a Prince
Talent and no energy you're a pauper.

With best wishes

Yours Sincerely

Jeffrey Archer

SIR CLEMENT ATHELSTON ARRINDELL, HE

GOVERNOR GENERAL OF ST CHRISTOPHER AND NEVIS

Sir Clement was born on 19 April 1931. He studied law and was called to the Bar at Lincoln's Inn, London in 1958. He has been a magistrate and a judge and was knighted in 1982.

It flatters me to think that as head of a tiny developing country I am being given a chance alongside the great philosophers and pundits who throughout the ages have essayed to set forth a credible thesis on the meaning and purpose of life.

This perplexing riddle threatens to outlast human existence itself, I believe. Are we the center-piece of all creation, the *magnum opus*, the *pièce de résistance*? Or are we merely accidental encrustations on a tiny planet hurtling around in space amidst giant planets, hapless observers of the awesome power and limitlessness of the universe? In my layman's view, the organism called man is much too tiny to ever finally conclude the debate on the origin of matter and our place in the cosmos.

Religionists with their pantheistic reasoning ascribe everything to an immortal anthropomorphic God and Creator, even though an explanation of who or what He is or whence He came seems lacking – understandably perhaps, since He must necessarily remain just beyond the comprehension of us His mortal progeny.

Evolutionists for their part gropingly expound about the gasses and specks of dust which, by accretion over aeons, have coalesced into masses of matter, then breaking apart in centrifugal frenzy, still today forming new planets and other cosmic bodies. (Likewise there is scant explanation here as how this gas and dust came to be there in the first place.) Then we see Darwinism taking over from this point, with a reasonable argument.

Religious conviction apart, this ignorance as to the how, when, where and why of our existence has left an enfeebling psychological void, possibly affecting unawares our deepest cerebral processes and outlook. The only certitude is that all in creation have a common genesis. This of course still leaves your question unanswered.

The recognition of a common origin, a shared biological fate and destiny, hardly appears to beneficially influence our behaviour as individuals or as nations. Instead, we give way to impulses and behaviour which betray us all as mere closet Darwinists. One result is that our wizardry in science and technology is surpassed only by our inhumanity to one another.

It may be a good thing that we continue to ask about the meaning of life. If anything, it may indicate that we have not yet dangerously settled into any smug self-serving conviction, or any paranoid mind-set, but rather that we open-mindedly remain in the market-place of ideas, whereby constant interchange might bring us one day to a fuller understanding and appreciation of ourselves and of one another. Understanding ought to be more helpful to the human organism, whatever its origin, than ignorance and mistrust.

B

Life is drawing sufficient conclusions from insufficient premises.

SAMUEL BUTLER

There are only three events in a man's life; birth, life, and death; he is not conscious of being born, he dies in pain, and he forgets to live.

JEAN DE LA BRUYÈRE

Life is too short for chess.

JAMES HENRY BYRON

MATTHEW BAGGOTT

SUPERINTENDENT – METROPOLITAN POLICE

Matthew was born in London in 1958. He has a degree in history and has been a policeman for his entire working life. He has served in a variety of jobs which have mainly been operational roles in the inner city.

Dear Sir,

Thank you for your letter of May 7th 1994 in which you invite the Commissioner to comment upon the 'meaning of life'. Regrettably, I am afraid that the sheer number of requests for his views means that he is unable to provide a contribution. Nevertheless he has asked me to wish you all success in your venture.

On a personal note I can quite understand your search for wisdom and answers, particularly when personal circumstances do not seem to fit with our long held beliefs or attitudes. I have always found the words of John's Gospel and Psalm 139 help to focus the mind. Whilst no-one is immune from suffering and explanation is difficult, I find great reassurance in the belief that love and goodness will always, ultimately triumph. Selflessness on behalf of others, is perhaps the finest quality of mankind.

I do hope that your search provides answers.

Yours sincerely,
Matthew Baggott
A/Superintendent
Staff Officer
to Commissioner

RONNIE BARKER, OBE

COMIC ACTOR

Ronnie was born on 25 September 1929. His acting career started in 1948 with the Aylesbury Repertory Company and his stage work includes Irma la Douce, On the Brighter Side *and* The Two Ronnies. *He has won many awards and is perhaps best known for his work in television on* The Two Ronnies, Porridge, Open All Hours *and* Clarence.

Dear Jonathan Gabay,

I don't think life has any meaning.

It has beauty, it has ugliness. It has happiness, and pain, love, hate, great rewards and sometimes enormous responsibilities. It has laughter.

But it has no meaning. A cowslip in the hedgerow doesn't *mean* anything, neither does a sunrise over a tropical sea, or a thunderstorm. They are wonders of Nature, but they don't mean anything.

If I had to give a short answer it would be 'Life is meaningless, but it is wonderful. Where would we be without it? You're dead right we would'.

Ronnie Barker

PROFESSOR MICHAEL BAUM, CHM, FRCS, MD

SURGEON (CANCER SPECIALIST)

Professor Baum was born in London on 31 May 1937. He was educated at the University of Birmingham. He is currently a consultant surgeon at the Royal Marsden Hospital NHS Trust, emeritus professor of surgery at the Institute of Cancer Research and a professor at University College London. Between 1980 and 1990 he was professor of surgery at King's College School of Medicine and Dentistry.

I welcome this opportunity to try to synthesise nearly 50 years of self questioning and life experience. Ten years ago I suffered a severe bout of clinical depression. Only fellow sufferers, including the editor of this book, will fully appreciate what this means. It is not simply a sensation of being down in the dumps or thoroughly pissed off with things, but a sense of utter worthlessness and bleak despair. No amount of reassurance from my family or friends could persuade me that I was of any worth and that my life had any meaning.

Towards the end of this illness I experienced an episode that can only be described as a sunburst of happiness and in a crude attempt to emulate Van Gogh I describe this feeling with a painting of sunflowers created with a palate knife and thick impasto. Although frightful at the time I think that period of illness was of enormous and lasting value to me. Many people live their life taking it for granted without truly valuing the gift.

There is no better way of describing my attitude to life than by using the words of George Bernard Shaw: 'This is the true joy in life, the being used for a purpose recognised by yourself as a mighty one, the being a force of nature instead of a feverish little clod of ailments and grievances complaining that the world will not devote itself to making you happy. I am of the opinion that my life belongs to the whole community, and as long as I live it is my privilege to do for it whatever I can. I want to be thoroughly used up when I die, for the harder I work the more I live. I rejoice in life for its own sake. Life is no brief candle to me. It is a sort of splendid torch which I have got hold of for the moment and I want to make it burn as brightly as possible before handing it on to future generations.'

LORD BELOFF

LIFE PEER

Lord Beloff was born on 2 July 1913. Between 1946 and 1956 he was an academic reader in the comparative study of institutions. He was also a professor of government and public administration. In addition to his duties in the House of Lords, he is an honorary professor at the University of St Andrews.

I find it odd as an octogenarian to be faced with a problem I have never considered. I would not even attempt to tackle it now were it not that I do not like refusing anything to the Red Cross whose work is one of the few hopeful features in a world beset with violence. The reason for not having asked myself this question is that like many people, I have taken the fact of being on this earth for granted and used my energies either to cope with the current problems of daily life, like earning a living for oneself and one's family, or with finding ways of filling with rewarding occupations such time as can be spared from the daily round.

For those who have contemplated such deep matters, two paths have suggested themselves. The most common one has been to assume a divine creator and believe that life is given its meaning by our obligation to follow His precepts. I find this a perfectly satisfactory answer and the traditions of my own (Jewish) religion enough for my purposes – it is clearly true of adherents of the other major world religions where the ethical content is often identical. The other path is that of natural science where we have to believe on evidence that most of us cannot test for ourselves and find difficult to grasp that life in general and human life in particular are the result of some cosmic accident bringing together a necessary combination of chemical substances in a suitable environment. Some people feel that the first answer cancels out the second – like the 'creationists' in the United States who accept Genesis literally; others believe that the second cancels out the first and that science and religion are conflicting versions of reality of which only 'science' is true. Some find that both sets of beliefs can be adhered to without any sense of inner conflict.

What all three groups would agree upon is that life itself particularly in its more advanced forms is basically a state of activity. Where human beings are concerned the questions that pose themselves daily are not questions of meaning but of conduct. As we look at other people – we are nearly all too lenient judges of ourselves – we see what it is that we admire and where we find them wanting. In that respect, the religious are at an advantage since they have codes of conduct which they may or may not observe but to which reference can always be made. It is hard to derive any code of action from the truths of natural science. If everything is the result of a fortuitous set of events in an ultimately unknowable universe and if human behaviour is 'all in the genes' there can be nothing to choose between Attila the Hun and St Francis of Assisi. None of this amounts to condemning the pursuit of natural science since the exploration of physical reality has always been seen as a praiseworthy human activity – discovering a new star like the composition of a new symphony seems praiseworthy on the face of it. Those of us who could do neither can only watch and applaud.

What we do know about human beings suggests that for most people what they see and implicitly accept as the meaning of life is a balance between furthering their own desires and contributing to the happiness of others whether within the narrow circle of families and friends or in a wider arena. But the application of this simple analysis becomes harder when we live in the more complex societies of our own times. The philosophers of the ancient world to whose thinking on such matters little of substance has been added were confronted with societies on a small scale, with limited subdivisions, and only occasionally and remotely affected by what went on elsewhere. None of this is true of the contemporary 'global village' – no wonder we find it hard to work out a rationale for conduct.

My own approach to much of the problem of conduct is given its bias by the two activities which have together taken up my adult life – the study, writing and teaching of history and some degree of immersion in national politics. One cannot derive 'the meaning of life' from history – and historians who have tried to do so have usually ended as false prophets. Yet unless one is aware of the variety of ways in which human beings have behaved and organised themselves one can do little to judge between the various courses of action recommended by the different schools of thought. The swings between utopian optimism and the deepest pessimism that seem to afflict societies and their leaders can only be corrected by a greater awareness of what gives rise or has given rise to particular forms of human behaviour.

War is bad, peace is good; cruelty is odious, compassion life-enhancing. Why then do we see a history of wars and revolutions almost always accompanied by the flourishing of cruelty and the absence of compassion? We might as well say that health is good and ill-health odious for the sufferer and those around him and ask why then do so many of us lead

17

unhealthy lives? One can try to understand motivation; one can fall back upon naturalistic explanations such as that war and massacres are nature's way of keeping a necessary check upon population – but it is better to accept ignorance. We need to grasp simple things such as that doing evil now so that good may come in the future – a belief that lies at the basis of most political ideologies – should always be challenged. All human contrivances are second best.

I do not think one should worry too much about whether we can or ever will attach a meaning to 'the meaning of life'. Let those who need the delights of paradise or the horrors of hell to persuade them to good actions have them on offer – let those of a more abstract turn of mind find other arguments to persuade them to do good. In the long run it comes to the same. Above all, do not pretend.

SIDNEY BENARDOUT, P PR AGDC, P PR JGD

FREEMASON AND RETIRED HAIRDRESSER

Sidney was born on 6 May 1911. He was brought up in east London. Sidney spent four years in the army and 47 years as a hairdresser. He became a worshipful master in freemasonry and was directly honoured for his work by Prince Michael of Kent. He is married and has two sons.

Dear Jonathan,

I give below a few words I have learnt throughout my life and in particular what Freemasonry has taught me in the last thirty years.

The Meaning of Life varies to some extent on the age group of each individual. At an early age in life, we try to achieve the most of a care free life. We then go on to a life of activity and try to achieve a position where our future will be determined and naturally work hard to get the best out of life. In middle age we try fervently to stabilise our position in order that we accomplish a reasonably happy and healthy retirement.

You are then face to face with reality and begin to think all is not well with the world at large. Wars are waged because of greed inherent in many people and in consequence of this many thousands of people are killed and others are left to starve to death. Freemasonry has always advocated that BY DOING UNTO OTHERS AS YOU WOULD WISH TO BE DONE TO YOU would be the ideal for every individual in the world and become the true Meaning Of Life which I strongly endorse.

Yours sincerely and fraternally,
W.Bro Sidney Benardout P Pr AGDC, P PR JGD
Lodge of Felicity No.7509

THE RT HON. TONY BENN, MP

POLITICIAN

Tony was born on 3 April 1925. He is the eldest son of the 1st Viscount Stansgate and was educated at Westminster School and New College, Oxford. Tony has been in politics since 1950. His many political achievements include recommending the establishment of the GPO as a public corporation. He was Minister of Technology 1966–70, assumed responsibility for the Ministry of Aviation in 1967 and was Opposition Spokesman on Trade and Industry from 1970 to 1974. He was made Secretary of State for Industry and Minister of Posts and Telecommunications in 1974 and the following year became Secretary of State for Energy. His books include Year of Hope – Diaries, Letters and Poems 1940–62, Arguments for Socialism *and* The Regeneration of Britain. *His contribution is an extract from* The Independent Mind, *the first of three lectures in a series entitled* Is There No Alternative? *which he delivered in 1993.*

My father had many sayings and one of them was, 'Dare to be a Daniel, dare to stand alone', and I have a picture of Daniel in the lion's den which I carry with me in my wallet.

If we are going to overcome the problems that now confront us, which are quite fundamental, it won't just be the choice of a political party or candidate or leader. It will involve us going a bit deeper into the moral basis of our decisions, the democratic structure under which we are governed, and the international aspects of every decision we take.

And perhaps for that purpose the Independent Mind might come in quite useful.

MAURICE BENZIMRA

SECRETARY TO THE BRITISH CONGREGATION OF SPANISH AND PORTUGUESE
JEWS

Maurice was born on 21 February 1928. He was educated in England and due to the sudden death of his father was responsible, from the age of sixteen, for bringing up his family of five. He devoted 51 years to the welfare of a religious congregation, including overseeing marriages, deaths and births. He retired to Dimona in Israel and at the age of 68 became grandfather to four grandchildren (all born within the space of a month!).

Life without meaning or purpose is meaningless. God created Adam and Eve who became the first human beings charged not just to fulfil but to enjoy the meaning of life. 'Be fruitful and multiply', the Almighty instructed.

But for the call of making life meaningful, the universe would have remained in a void state following creation. The human race soon appreciated the meaning of life and went to immeasurable lengths to safeguard and protect it.

The individual, consciously or subconsciously, cherishes the meaning of life; every action he/she performs is so motivated. True, evil has as much a share in the meaning of life as goodness. They are both equally meaningful but it's the individual who determines which direction to take.

History shows that ultimately goodness prevails over evil and the world today would be even better served if greater exertions were placed to achieve and enjoy the good aspects of the meaning of life, collectively and individually. It was the prophet Micah who summed up the meaning of life so simply and majestically.

'What does the Lord require of thee? Only to do justly, to love mercy and to walk humbly.'

ANTON BERG

SPIRITUALIST

Anton was born in Hampstead, London in 1934. He describes himself as a World War II blitz child. He is Jewish but found joy in spiritualism as a natural clairvoyant and healer. He is now retired from his main career, which was printing, but still likes to 'keep in touch' in other areas.

The meaning of life, what a question! Scientists, theologians and just about everyone in the known world must have asked that question and do they have an answer? No! Probably like me just a belief. The present scientific answer rests on the big bang creation of the universe. What I want to know is who or what created what led to the big bang. I might just as well ask for proof of UFOs. Most religions believe in God or at least someone like him, that is if he is a he. Again no proof but neither can anyone disprove it either. Others believe you are born, you live and you die, with nothing in between. That theory I cannot subscribe to.

So what is the answer? For many years now for want of anything else I have believed in Spiritualism. Not as a religion but something that makes more sense than most other beliefs to me. The so-called gift of being a medium is supposedly mine. Not fortune telling, nothing for the future. It relates to being able to communicate with a person who is grieving or is troubled. This is when it manifests itself. Somehow the ability to bring back memories of other people or possessions that can be of comfort. Another is to see in people the ability to heal and to enable them to understand and practise that particular gift, otherwise known as faith-healing. How does it work? God only knows! My own theory is that the brain is a transmitter/receiver and is able to communicate with other brains and delve into memory banks to see a picture or thought there. Yes, I do appreciate that this can also be nonsense and is unproved but do you have a better idea.

I also believe that we have several stages of existence, rather like an apprenticeship. That this life serves as a means to a better life yet to come. That one has to suffer oneself to be able to appreciate the suffering of others. Now that ties in nicely with many other religious views. My further belief is that we are here to help and support others. I constantly ask myself like everyone else in the world, why? I have lived through the Second World War. The Holocaust. Every day there is famine, murder, war and mayhem thrust at us through the media. I suffer bad health

22

myself and see family and friends go through hell just like you do. How can anyone in their right mind believe in God or anything else with all of this still going on in a modern so-called civilised world? Yet I do. Always there is that intuition, the belief that there is something better ahead, that this is a passing phase. Many people seem instinctively to know that they have lived before. Why do some have wisdom and others not? Who decides who will be rich and another poor. Questions always questions with no answers, just an instinctive belief that others call faith.

One thing I do know is that I am not alone. There are many carers in the world. Angels who give their time, their careers, sometimes their own lives to help others. Have they all got it wrong? No, there just has to be something beyond what we know for the present. In the meantime, thank God, whoever or whatever that is perceived as being. The majority of the human race does care, there are nurses, doctors and organisations who believe that life does have a meaning and are prepared to back that belief with their own.

HELENA BONHAM-CARTER

ACTRESS

Helena was born on 26 May 1966. Her father, Raymond Bonham-Carter, was executive director of S.G. Warburg & Co. He retired in 1979 after being disabled. Helena's films include A Room with a View, Hamlet, Frankenstein *and* Getting It Right, *and she has starred in* Miami Vice *and* The Darling Buds of May *on television. Her theatre work includes* The Barber of Seville *and* Women in White.

Dear Jonathan,

Thank you for your letter asking for my opinion on 'the meaning of life'. Tough question and one that I must confess to not having a definitive answer – surprise, surprise!

One idea that occurred to me is that 'meaning' is a human construct of ours, trapped by our inability to think in any other way than in terms of logic, we therefore need to search for 'meaning' when perhaps there is none to be found.

In the absence of any satisfactory theory of my own, I will borrow the wisdom of Joseph Campbell, a man who did seem to have all the answers. He said something to the effect that 'it is not the meaning of life which we pursue, but the *experience of being alive* – the rapture of it'. The exact quote can be found at the beginning of the 'Power of the Myth' by Joseph Campbell.

I hope this is of help and good luck with your search for the answer to the big question.

Helena Bonham-Carter

BOUTROS BOUTROS-GHALI, PhD

SECRETARY-GENERAL OF THE UNITED NATIONS

Dr Boutros-Ghali was born on 14 November 1922. Before being given one of the world's most responsible positions, he was a professor of international law and international relations and head of the department of political science at Cairo University. He has also been Minister of State of Foreign Affairs in Egypt and Deputy Prime Minister for Foreign Affairs. His publications include Foreign Policies in a World of Change.

Dear Mr Gabay,

I am writing, on behalf of the Secretary-General, in response to your letter of 11 September 1994.

The Secretary-General's definition of the meaning of life is to be fully committed to one's ideals. A meaningful life, for the Secretary-General, is a life that is lived to the utmost of all possibilities, notwithstanding limitations.

Yours sincerely,
Mourad Wahba
Senior Officer

THE RT HON. SIR RHODES BOYSON, MP

POLITICIAN

Sir Rhodes was born on 11 May 1925. He was educated at the University of Manchester and at Cambridge (BA, MA, PhD). He has been a headmaster of various schools and entered national politics in 1970. He is MP (Conservative) for Brent North.

MEMBER OF PARLIAMENT FOR BRENT NORTH

HOUSE OF COMMONS
LONDON SW1A 0AA

5th July 1994.

Dear Jonathan,

It is always good to hear from you.

My philosophy of life is to get up early, face front and battle on all sides for what one believes in and for ones friends, and in my case, constituents!

All good wishes.

Yours sincerely,

Rhodes

The Rt. Hon. Dr.Sir Rhodes Boyson, MP

BRAINS

INVENTOR OF THUNDERBIRD VEHICLES

Brains is the genius inventor of International Rescue's Thunderbird vehicles. He was created by puppeteer Sylvia Anderson (to whom he told the following meaning of life). Famous for his oversized glasses, without Brains the good citizens of earth would be no more than puppets to the evil hood.

Dear Jonathan:

The meaning of life is searching for the meaning of life. And would somebody please bring me to life! (As told to Sylvia Anderson.)

Yours truly,
Brains

Thunderbirds © TM 1994 ITC Entertainment Group Ltd

JANET BROWN

ACTRESS AND COMEDIENNE

Janet was born in Glasgow and is one of the UK's best known comediennes. She has won the TV Times *Funniest Woman on TV Award and the Pye Colour TV Award. Her television work includes* Meet Janet Brown *and* Janet and Co. *and she has appeared in films such as* For Your Eyes Only *and* Flood Tide.

JANET BROWN

June 20, 1994

Dear Mr Gabay,

      I found your question such an enormous one that I put it to one side. But having read your letter again, I am sending my reply in the hope that it goes some way towards helping.

      Basically I feel that life is here to be lived, appreciated and to know that we are, in spite of appearances at times, expressing good and this good is the <u>real</u> life. Does that make sense! I do hope so.

      I send my best wishes to you and your family and hope that doors are opening up for you.

      Yours sincerely,

Janet Brown

C

I am the Light of the World. He that followeth me walketh not in darkness, but shall have the light of life.

JESUS CHRIST

Life is a maze in which we take the wrong turning before we have learnt to walk.

CYRIL CONNOLLY

Tzu-kung asked about the true gentleman. The Master said, 'He does not preach what he practises till he practises what he preaches.'

CONFUCIUS

Life is a tragedy when seen in close-up, but a comedy in long-shot.

SIR CHARLIE CHAPLIN

FRANK CARSON

COMEDIAN

Frank was born in Belfast on 6 November 1926. His catchphrase, 'It's the way I tell 'em' has gone down in comedy folklore. His charity work has earned him the honour of Knight of the Grand Cross of St Gregory, awarded by Pope John Paul II. His television work includes The Comedians, Noel's House Party *and* Tiswas.

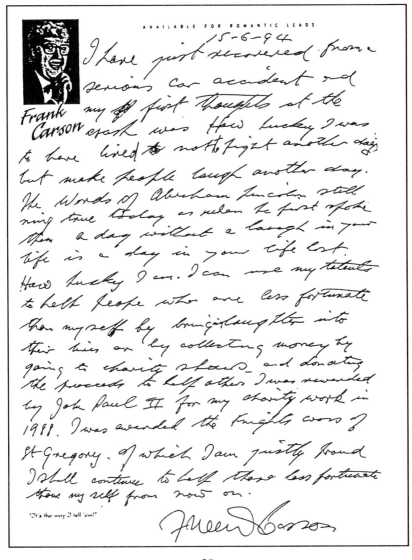

AVAILABLE FOR ROMANTIC LEADS

15-6-94

Frank Carson

I have just recovered from a serious car accident and my first thoughts at the crash was How lucky I was to have lived to not to fight another day but make people laugh another day. The Words of Abraham Lincoln still ring true today as when he first spoke them a day without a laugh in your life is a day in your life lost. How lucky I am. I can use my talents to help people who are less fortunate than myself by bringing laughter into their lives or by collecting money by going to charity shows and donating the proceeds to help others. I was rewarded by John Paul II for my charity work in 1981. I was awarded the Knights cross of St Gregory. Of which I am justly proud. I shall continue to help those less fortunate than my self from now on.

"It's the way I tell 'em!"

ROY CASTLE, OBE

TV PRESENTER, SINGER, DANCER, ACTOR, COMEDIAN, MUSICIAN AND GUINNESS
WORLD RECORD BREAKER

Roy submitted his contribution to this book just a couple of months before he sadly died from lung cancer (thought to have been contracted from passive smoking). His was the first contribution I received.

Roy first worked on stage with comedians such as Norman Teal, Jimmy Clitheroe and Jimmy James and went on to present Record Breakers *and the BAFTA award-winning* All Star Record Breakers. *Roy held two Guinness world records: tap dancing (completing one million taps in 23 hours 45 minutes) and wing walking from Gatwick to Paris (in 3 hours 23 minutes).*

1. 3. 94

Dear Jonathan

Thanks so much for the letter inviting me to contribute to your book.

My answer to the question "What is the meaning of life?" is - **Love God and all that he created - to be able, as the end comes to look back and smile.**

I hope this is suitable for you and that your book is a success.

All the best

Roy Castle

CHILDREN, AGED TWO, THREE AND FOUR, FROM THE KINGSBURY JEWISH KINDERGARTEN IN LONDON

ARTHUR C. CLARKE, CBE

AUTHOR, SCIENTIST, LECTURER

Arthur was born on 16 December 1917 in Minehead, Somerset, and worked in scientific research before turning to fiction. His fascination with exploration and space resulted in some of the most famous science fiction books of the twentieth century. Many have been made into films such as 2001: A Space Odyssey *and its sequel,* 2010. *Today Arthur is considered as one of the world's leading lecturers and authors in his field.*

If decades and centuries pass with no indication that there is intelligent life elsewhere in the universe, the long-term effects on human philosophy will be profound, and may be disastrous. Better to have neighbours we don't like than to be utterly alone. For that cosmic loneliness could point to a very depressing conclusion: that intelligence marks an evolutionary dead end. When we consider how well the sharks and cockroaches have managed without it, and how badly we are managing *with* it, one cannot help wondering if intelligence is an aberration like the armour of the dinosaurs, dooming its possessors to extinction.

No, I don't *really* believe this. Even if the computers we carry on our shoulders are evolutionary accidents, they can now generate their own programs – and set their own goals.

For we can now say, in the widest possible meaning of the phrase, that the purpose of human life is information processing. I have already mentioned the strange fact that men can survive longer without water than without information. And therefore the real value of all the devices we have been discussing is that they have the potential for immensely enriching and enlarging life, by giving us more information to process – up to the maximum number of bits per second that the human brain can absorb.

I am happy, therefore, to have solved one of the great problems the philosophers and theologians have been haggling over for several thousand years. You may, perhaps, feel that this is rather a dusty answer, and that not even the most inspired preacher could even found a religion upon the slogan: 'The purpose of life is information processing.' Indeed, you may even retort, 'Well, what is the purpose of information processing?'

I'm glad you asked me that.

C. JOHN CLIFFORD

WARDEN OF THE OXFORD UNIVERSITY GUILD SOCIETY

John was born on 5 February 1932. He was once a novice Benedictine monk. After a period in the monastery he entered the world of fine wines and became manager of marketing services for Moët and Chandon (London) Ltd. He is also a member of the General Council of the Wine and Spirit Association of Great Britain and Northern Ireland.

Life is for living with meaning and purpose,
With verity, charity, mercy and fun,
And guidance and strength down the pathway eternal,
From Jehovah our father and Jesus, his son.

JOHN CONTEH

FORMER PROFESSIONAL BOXER

John was born in Liverpool on 27 May 1951. He has had seven light to heavyweight world title fights. He won four and lost three. In 1970 he won the Commonwealth middleweight title and in 1974 the world light-heavyweight title.

4/8/94

Dear Jonathan,

I think the meaning of life is that while we are here, we are to learn the spiritual lessons.

yours faithfully

John Conteh

DAME CATHERINE COOKSON, DBE

NOVELIST

Catherine was born on 20 June 1906 in County Durham. She is one of the world's bestselling authors and many of her books have been made into TV mini-dramas. Her publications include Kate Hannigan, Maggie Rowan, Our Kate *(autobiographical),* The Dwelling Place *and* The Glass Virgin.

Dame Catherine Cookson D.B.E., D. Litt., M.A.

31st May, 1994.

Dear Mr. Gabay,

    Dame Catherine has been unwell for some time now, and unfortunately, at eighty-seven, she is fast losing her sight. Consequently, I am having to answer her mail.

    Mrs. Cookson is in her 88th year and is almost blind, and she says, "In answer, sir, to your unintelligent question, if I knew the meaning of Life I would have been the creator of it."

Yours sincerely,

Sarah A. Sables(Secretary).

COOMBS, PAT

ACTRESS

Pat was born in London on 27 August 1930. She trained at LAMDA, where she subsequently taught drama. She has starred in films such as Ooh . . . You Are Awful *and* Adolf Hitler – My Part in his Downfall *and her television work includes* Eastenders, Noel's House Party *and* You're Only Young Twice.

Dear Jonathan Gabay,

I have your recent letter to hand and only wish I knew how to answer your Burning Question!!

It isn't that I haven't thought about THE MEANING OF LIFE . . . I have – many, many times – (haven't we all?) and, still, I don't honestly know the answer(s).

I can only tell you that, from a very early age, I appreciated and understood the love of 'family' and that for me, personally, family love and understanding would carry me through. I like to think it has! Simplistic? YES! As indeed are my thoughts about religion, relationships, work, ambition, politics and almost anything else you care to name.

I think most of us, at some time or another, feel we may have lost our sense of direction . . . and we look back and wonder *why?* Things we thought so important – things we thought so essential for our well-being . . . as I once considered marriage and children to be – 'twas *not* to be! But it has never altered my love of children and my acceptance of what life can and *does* do to you . . . The losses, the gains, the fun, the tears, the joy – and 'specially (for me!) the laughter! Plus the company of puss-cats. I'm *sure* I was put here for a purpose and I hope so much that it was to bring a smile to someone, somewhere – *IF* I HAVE SUCCEEDED THEN, FOR ME, THAT *IS* THE MEANING OF LIFE.

Sincerely,
Pat Coombs

D

Know thyself.

ORACLE OF DELPHI

To love the Lord that is your life and length of days.

DEUTERONOMY

DALAI LAMA (TENZIN GYATSO)

TEMPORAL AND SPIRITUAL HEAD OF TIBET; FOURTEENTH INCARNATION

The Dalai Lama was born on 6 July 1935. He was enthroned at Lhasa in 1940 but his rights were exercised by a regency until 1950. After fleeing to Chumbi in South Tibet, he assumed political power in 1950. He was awarded the Congressional Human Rights Award and the Nobel Peace Prize in 1989 and the Freedom Award (USA) in 1991. His publications include My Land and People *and* Freedom in Exile.

One great question underlies our experience, whether we think about it consciously or not: What is the purpose of life? I have considered this question and would like to share my thoughts in the hope that they may be of direct, practical benefit to those who read them.

I believe that the purpose of life is to be happy. From the moment of birth, every human being wants happiness and does not want suffering. Neither social conditioning nor education nor ideology affect this. From the very core of our being, we simply desire contentment. I don't know whether the universe, with its countless galaxies, stars and planets, has a deeper meaning or not, but at the very least, it is clear that we humans who live on this earth face the task of making a happy life for ourselves. Therefore, it is important to discover what will bring about the greatest degree of happiness.

DENNIS THE MENACE

CARTOON CHEEKY SCHOOLBOY

Dennis was born on 17 March 1951 in the comic Beano *on page five. His first headline was, 'Look! Here's a new pal you'll enjoy – he's the world's wildest boy.' In 1968, he was joined by his best friend Gnasher, an extremely rare Abyssinian wire-haired tripe hound. The Dennis the Menace Fan Club and Gnasher Fang Club have in excess of 1,000,000 members to date.*

JAMIE DOW

CONSUMER PSYCHOLOGIST

Jamie has a first class honours degree in psychology and has tutored in psychology, research techniques and statistics to university undergraduates. He has held several important senior advertising agency planning positions and is responsible for helping some of the world's leading brands to effectively implement their marketing strategies.

Life isn't so much a case of what happens to you because, to a certain extent at least, this is beyond your control.

Rather, it's a question of how you respond to events and, related to this, whether you're happy with the way that you react.

Most people tend to be unhappy when they hold a mirror up to themselves.

Don't take on so.

Try to resist the temptation to totally reinvent yourself.

Rather, first recognise, and then learn to love, your strengths, ie those aspects of your personality which you feel help you to manage the overall process of change and individual episodes within it.

Simply be aware of the more negative, ie less helpful, aspects of your personality because to be forewarned is to be forearmed.

And whenever the going threatens to get too tough, steel yourself with this one thought: You've got this far, so there can't be that much wrong with you.

JUDGE DREDD

CARTOON LAWMASTER

Born in 1971, with the catchphrase, 'He's the law – and you better believe it,' 'His Honour' Judge Dredd became a top cult hero in the eighties. In the nineties he was brought to life in the Hollywood blockbuster movie Judge Dredd, *starring Sylvester Stallone.*

I stand for justice. I stand for discipline, good order and the rigid application of the Law – and Grud help any limp-wrist liberals who say any different.

Judge Dredd and all associated characters and settings copyright © Egmont H. Petersen Ford, Gutenberghus ⊙ Licensed by Copyright Promotions Ltd.

E

The man who regards his life and that of his fellow creatures as meaningless is not merely unhappy but hardly fit for life.

ALBERT EINSTEIN

Seek not good from without: seek it within yourselves, or you will never find it.

EPICURUS

Live life to the full. Have fun or it all falls apart.

KENNY EVERETT

CHRISTOPHER EUBANK

PROFESSIONAL BOXER

Chris was born on 8 August 1966. His professional boxing début was in 1985. Titles won include the WBC middleweight and the WBO middleweight in 1990 and the WBO super-middleweight in 1991. He has in excess of 36 professional wins to his credit.

The meaning of life is to do good, emulate good, epitomise good, to reflect it.

The meaning of life is to do good and not the opposite.

EDGAR EVANS

FORMER PRINCIPAL TENOR AT THE NEW COVENT GARDEN OPERA COMPANY

Edgar was born in Cardiganshire on 9 June 1912. He is the son of a farmer and the youngest of thirteen children. He studied with a professor from the Royal College of Music. During the Second World War, he sang for the troops at over 500 concerts. In 1946 he joined the New Covent Garden Opera Company and has been hailed by the critics as 'remarkable'.

Life is what you make of it.

Looking back on my life it was never easy. Fortunately I was born with a God given voice, and a one track mind to go with it – to be a 1st class singer. It was the only gift I ever had and I made it to where I always wanted to be. A Principal Tenor at the Royal Opera House, Covent Garden, which I held for nearly 30 years. On retiring I became Professor of vocal technique at the Royal College of Music passing on to budding singers the way, many of whom have reached high standards.

In conclusion, take my advice. If you have a talent stick to it, never deviate, make it your main interest apart of course, from survival which is inherent in all life.

P.S. I would love to do it all over again.

PROFESSOR H. J. EYSENCK, PhD, DSc

PROFESSOR EMERITUS OF PSYCHOLOGY

Hans was born on 4 March 1916 in Berlin, Germany. Between 1942 and 1945 he was a research psychologist at Mill Hill Emergency Hospital. He then became a psychologist at Maudsley Hospital, London. His publications include Uses and Abuses of Psychology, Decline and Fall of the Freudian Empire *and* Know Your Own IQ.

One often assumes that if a question can be asked, there must be an answer to it. This is not so. Science is the source of our most reliable answers, but only in response to 'how?' questions; it is silent when confronted with 'why?' questions. Newton's formulae answers very adequately the question of *how* two masses attract each other, but neither he nor Einstein or anyone else can answer the question of *why* they should do so, or why they should obey his laws. It is often useful, when considering a question, to think just what sort of a reply could possibly answer that question. Often it will be clear that there just is no possible answer to that question; or that any answer would be merely begging the question. We can say that masses attract each other in proportion to their weight, and the distance between them, because God ordained it. But why did God ordain it? Every answer to a *why* question leads to another why question, in infinite regression.

The question about the meaning of life is such a *why* question; in the nature of things it can have no answer because it is not a *how* question. In so far as it can be made a *how* question (how did we get here in the first place?) these are some answers – big bang, evolution, survival of the fittest. But that merely postulates random events following universal laws that know no why. Religion attempts to give meaning to life, in terms of certain values, human relations, beliefs. But these are self-validating – you may believe or not. And your likelihood of belief is itself determined largely by genetic factors; we literally inherit our propensity for religious belief (or disbelief!). Having inherited the latter, I find it difficult to accept religious answers to the why question.

Essentially I would think that while there is no meaningful *universal*, scientifically verifiable answer, each person has an individual, personalised answer in terms of his *heredity* and his personal environment, his history of reinforcement, as Skinner puts it. You are an epicurean or a stoic, a hero or a coward, selfish or altruistic, because of who you are, and what

45

happens to you; you express your belief about the meaning of life through your actions. These are not conscious decisions, based on philosophical or scientific premises (although we may flatter ourselves that they are in our case!); they are summaries of habits acquired and directions inherited. In other words, life has meaning in a *general* sense, but it has a certain meaning for me personally, a meaning that I express through my actions, my system of values, my general philosophy of life. But my sense of meaning will not be your sense of meaning, and there would be little sense in arguing who is right – by definition there can be no absolute answer!

F

This is the rule of and way of life . . . to observe the holy Gospel of our Lord Jesus Christ, living in obedience, without personal possessions, and in chastity.

ST FRANCIS OF ASSISI

Were it offered to my choice, I should have no objections to a repetition of the same life from its beginning, only asking the advantages authors have in a second edition to correct some faults of the first.

BENJAMIN FRANKLIN

The goal of all life is death.

SIGMUND FREUD

DOUGLAS FAIRBANKS JUNIOR, KBE, DSc

ACTOR

Douglas was born in New York City on 9 December 1909. Between 1922 and 1924 he studied painting and sculpture in Paris. He became a film actor in 1923, began writing professionally in 1928 and started his own production company in the UK in 1935. His films include Stella Dallas, Sinbad the Sailor *and* A Woman of Affairs. *He has produced over 160 TV plays and wrote his biography,* The Salad Days, *in 1988.*

Douglas Fairbanks, Jr.
Inverness Counsel

September 16, 1994

Dear Mr. Gabay,

I cannot imagine a more provocative, more profound but frustrating question than the one you have posed - "What is the Meaning of Life?" If the ancient Egyptians and early Greeks were as absorbed by the question as the records show they were, and yet failed to come up with a universally acceptable answer, then what credentials do I have which could hope to succeed?

Perhaps there is no answer - only a reply. That reply could be "Does Life <u>have</u> to have a meaning?" And if so, why? It is possible that in the great scheme of the universe of some milliards of light years spreading in all directions everything "just happened" - without rhyme or reason. It is also possible that there was no beginning (if one stops to think that one out, one could go crazy!). Even the great Professor Einstein called <u>his</u> answer a "theory."

I would go on but I would risk boring you and neglecting my business. Thank you for writing. I look forward to reading how others have answered your query.

Sincerely,

Douglas Fairbanks, Jr.

SIR RANULPH FIENNES, OBE, DSc

EXPLORER

Sir Ranulph is one of the world's great adventurers. Educated at Eton, he was the leader of six major expeditions between 1969 and 1986, including a journey up the White Nile by hovercraft and parachuting on to the Jostedal glacier in Norway. Between 1979 and 1982 he organised the Transglobe Expedition which traced the Greenwich Meridian, crossing both Poles. In 1990 he won the ITN Award for Event of the Decade.

Sir Ranulph Fiennes Bt. OBE DSc.

25 · 5 · 94

Dear Mr Gabay,

What's the Meaning of Life?

The Meaning of Life is of course very different to each individual. To me life has many meanings depending on what mood I'm in at the time.

Best Wishes

Ran Fiennes

Westward Ho Adventure Holidays Ltd. Directors: Sir Ranulph Fiennes Bt., Lady Fiennes
Incorporated 1966. VAT No. 391-3601-60. Registered Office: 339 Upper Street, London N1 0PD

DAPHNE FINER

FORMER BRITISH RED CROSS VOLUNTEER

Daphne was born in 1916. She was brought up in the East End of London and was a member of her local British Red Cross Society in Hendon, London for over twenty years. Today her daughter and grandson are members.

What is the meaning of life? This question, I believe, would evoke a very varied response, depending, as I believe it does, on the age, the character and the circumstances of those being questioned.

Let us take the ages of man, the child, the adolescent, the adult. The child would give little heed to this subject. He would be concerned only with the material things of life, his comforts, his pastimes, his activities, his well-being. The adolescent, possibly at an introspective stage might give it a little more thought. The adult, as the years go on, will evolve a multitude of theories.

I do not believe that it is a question which can be answered by one solution, by one train of thought. There are too many 'imponderables' as the saying goes, circumstances vary so much. The child brought up in a war-torn country and the child reared with every conceivable comfort; the person with robust health and the chronic invalid. These people would understandably have very differing views on the meaning of life. The severely handicapped ask 'Why, why me?' I think it was Goethe who said, 'Suffering enobles the human spirit'. However brave, however religious, surely, even if not voiced aloud the question arises, 'Why, why me?'

In yesterday's *Daily Telegraph*, there was an account of a missionary nurse, who, through no fault or misbehaviour of her own, had contracted Aids and had but little time left to live. The following is an excerpt from her personal account:

'. . . I am trying to understand God's purpose in giving me this to deal with. I came here [Nyange Zimbabwe] to help and I am thankful that I have been able to do this . . . Sometimes I do ask God "Why me?", but I am not bitter. I believe he put me through this to help other people to be more compassionate and to make me a better person.' Has this very courageous person answered the question in her own way?

ALAN FLETCHER

DESIGNER AND FOUNDING PARTNER, PENTAGRAM DESIGN

Alan was born in Nairobi, Kenya on 27 September 1931. His education included time spent at Yale University. He was a designer in the late 1950s for Fortune *magazine in New York, and ran his own design freelance practice in London between 1959 and 1962. He was a partner at Fletcher Forbes Gill and Crosby Fletcher Forbes before becoming a founding partner of Pentagram, one of the world's leading design companies.*

Dear Mr Fletcher.

I am working on a book for the British Red Cross working overseas. However I can't complete my project without *your* written answer to the following question: WHAT IS THE MEANING OF LIFE?

The book, The Meaning of Life is planned for publication in 1995 - the 125th birthday year of the British Red Cross. The book will feature answers to that question from notable people of all walks of life.

What made me embark on this project?

At the age of thirty-one, following employment, health and stress problems, I hit rock bottom. So I asked, for the sake of my three year old son, *'What is the meaning of life'*? That's how I started work on what was to become a fascinating and I believe very worthwhile book project - The Meaning of Life.

All royalties from the book will go directly to the British Red Cross for work throughout the world as well as the UK. The Red Cross's unique status and role under international law allows it to act as a neutral intermediary in humanitarian matters to protect and assist the victims of armed conflicts and internal disturbances.

You, I am sure will appreciate that without your help there wouldn't be a book. So thanks for your time in answering this question to help the British Red Cross give people the chance to live and enjoy life to the full.

Yours sincerely

Jonathan Gabay
PS Your answer should be sent to the address on this letter - not the Red Cross.

creativity

29
XI
94

FRED FLINTSTONE

CARTOON CAVEMAN, PHILOSOPHER AND CONSTRUCTION WORKER

Fred is one of the world's most popular cartoon characters. The Flintstones *is translated into 53 languages and seen each week by over 300 million people in 89 countries. In 1994, Fred and his modern stone age family were the subject of one of that year's highest-grossing box office movies –* The Flintstones.

As I always say to Barney, the meaning of life is to treat people right and love your family. Get it right and you'll have a yabba-Dabba-Doo time!

Fred Flintstone

BRYAN FORBES

ACTOR, WRITER AND FILM DIRECTOR

Bryan was born on 22 July 1926. He entered the acting profession in 1942. In 1959 he formed Beaver Films with Sir Richard Attenborough, and wrote and co-produced The Angry Silence *in 1960. He has written, directed and produced numerous films including* Only Two Can Play, Whistle Down the Wind, Better Late Than Never *and* The Naked Face. *He won the British Academy Award in 1960 and the Writers Guild Award twice. His publications include* Truth Lies Sleeping *and* The Distant Laughter.

To Jonathan Gabay,

I wish I knew the meaning of life. I suspect that for enormous numbers of people throughout the world life is one endless struggle from the cradle to the grave. Without being unduly cynical I am sure they are forced to agree with Flaubert's maxim that '*we shall find life tolerable once we have consented to be always ill at ease*'. The chasm between those who have and those who do not has never been bridged, and all the religions of the world have a lot to answer for. They have contributed in no small measure to the sum total of human misery.

Bryan Forbes

JAMES FOX

ACTOR

James was born William Fox on 19 May 1939. He entered acting as a child in 1950 but left to pursue a Christian vocation in 1970. He served in the armed forces between 1959 and 1961. He returned to acting full time in 1980. His films include The Servant, The Chase, A Passage to India, Farewell to the King *and* The Remains of the Day.

Dear Jonathan Gabay,

Thank you for your letter ref: What is the meaning of life? The fact that man must ask this question tells us two things:

One, that he is probably both unknowledgeable and insecure about his status here on earth.

Two, that he must believe there is an answer, in that he desires to ask the question, and hopes for an answer. I don't recall that Jesus was asked this question (perhaps it is a more Greek than Hebrew type of question), but he was questioned about the meaning of life in the sense, what *is* life?

And in my understanding, in John's gospel, at least, it is one of the *major* themes. And he answered the question, as you know, in many different ways, possibly to give it the fullest sense and meaning. Exploring this question with him as the source of its solution, I found it helpful to learn from him that there is both physical and spiritual birth (life) and one needs both to understand the meaning of life.

Yours,
James Fox

G

Life is a jest, and all things show it. I thought so once, but now I know it.
JOHN GAY (EPITAPH)

Life is a hereditary disease.
GRAFFITI SPOTTED IN LONDON

Life is but a constant dying.
MOSES GENTILI

It is the look in the eyes of a child who suddenly realises the importance of his or her life in the great scheme of things that brings meaning to my own life.
JANE GOODALL

ISAAC GABAY, MBE

FORMER EXECUTIVE CHEF OF THE HOUSE OF COMMONS

Isaac was born on the border of Spain and Gibraltar on 14 May 1931. He was educated in Tangier, Morocco. He started work as a kitchen boy in North Africa at the age of twelve and during the mid 1950s he joined the Royal Army Catering Corps. After completing his service he worked at several leading catering establishments until he was recruited as head chef for the British Parliament. He was awarded an MBE for 22 years of outstanding service.

The meaning of life.

The meaning of life depends on each individual. The important thing is to make the best of life each day and to give it its full value.

SIR JOHN GIELGUD

ACTOR

Sir John was born on 14 April 1904. His first stage appearance was at the Old Vic in 1921 and he became a leading Shakespearian actor of the British theatre. He has directed a number of productions, including Private Lives *and* The Last Joke *and he has also appeared in many films, notably as Cassius in* Julius Caesar. *He published his autobiography,* An Actor in his Time, *in 1979.*

Dear Jonathan Gabay,

How can we possibly know what life means? Or death either. Even the great geniuses of literature have failed to tell us. 'When we are born we cry that we have come to this great stage of fools.'
'Life's but a walking shadow – a poor player
that struts and frets his hour upon the stage
and then is heard no more. It is a tale
told by an idiot – full of sound and fury,
signifying nothing.'

John Gielgud

56

ÁRPÁD GÖNCZ, PhD

PRESIDENT OF HUNGARY

Árpád was born on 10 February 1922 in Budapest. He began his career as a banking clerk and then joined the Smallholders, Landworkers and Bourgeois Party. In 1958 he was sentenced to life imprisonment as a political defendant. Luckily he was released under amnesty in 1963. He then became a freelance writer and politician and has won various literary prizes including the Attila József Price. He has been President of Hungary since 1990.

A MAGYAR KÖZTÁRSASÁG
ELNÖKE

PRESIDENT OF THE REPUBLIC
OF HUNGARY

Budapest, October 3, 1994

Dear Mr. Gabay,

I would like to thank you for your letter of September 11 about your thoughtfull book planned for publication in 1995 with the assistance of the British Red Cross. I feel deeply honored to be invited to contribute to the noble aims of your project and the work of the Red Cross.

My definition for the meaning of life is: **the life itself.**

I wish you all the best and hope for the success of this project and your noble efforts,

Sincerely,

/ Árpád Göncz /

GRAHAM GOOCH, OBE

CRICKETER

Graham was born on 23 July 1953. He is a right hand batsman and a right arm medium bowler. His début for Essex was in 1973 and his test début came two years later. He captained the unofficial English XI in the South Africa tour in 1982 and consequently was banned from representing England for three years. He achieved over 30,000 career runs in July 1990 and is the only batsman to have scored a triple hundred and a hundred in the same match (England v. India at Lords in 1990). He has been captain of Essex since 1986 and captained the English team in July 1988 and between 1989 and 1993.

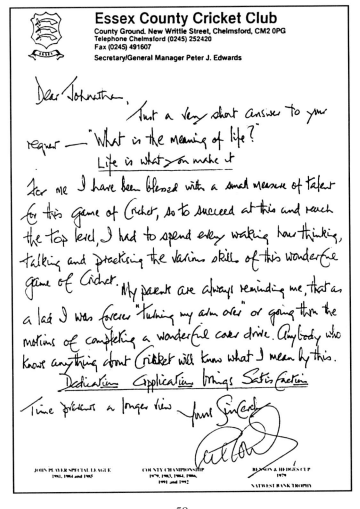

Essex County Cricket Club
County Ground, New Writtle Street, Chelmsford, CM2 0PG
Telephone Chelmsford (0245) 252420
Fax (0245) 491607
Secretary/General Manager Peter J. Edwards

Dear Johnathan,

Just a very short answer to your request — "What is the meaning of life?"

Life is what you make it

For me I have been blessed with a small measure of talent for this game of Cricket, so to succeed at this and reach the top level, I had to spend every waking hour thinking, talking and practising the various skills of this wonderful game of Cricket. My parents are always reminding me, that as a lad I was forever "turning my arm over" or going thro the motions of completing a wonderful cover drive. Anybody who knows anything about Cricket will know what I mean by this.

Dedication Application brings Satisfaction

Time prevents a longer view

Yours Sincerely

JOHN PLAYER SPECIAL LEAGUE
1981, 1984 and 1985

COUNTY CHAMPIONSHIP
1979, 1983, 1984, 1986,
1991 and 1992

BENSON & HEDGES CUP
1979

NATWEST BANK TROPHY

DR BILLY GRAHAM

EVANGELIST

Dr Graham was born on 7 November 1918. He was ordained to the Baptist ministry in 1940 and became the Hon. Chairman at the Lausanne Congress on World Evangelisation in 1974. During 1995 he took the message of the gospel to over 165 countries via satellite. This was the largest evangelical outreach in the history of the church. Numerous awards include the Bernard Baruch Award in 1955, the Man of the South Award in 1974 and the William Booth Award in 1985. Seventeen publications include Peace with God, The Jesus Generation *and* Till Armageddon.

Let me tell you where we are and what we are. We are a nation of empty people. Our heads are crammed full of knowledge, but within our souls is a spiritual vacuum.

Hundreds of philosophies and scores of religions have been invented by men in their efforts to circumvent the Word of God. Modern philosophers and psychologists are still trying to make it appear that there is some way out other than the path of Jesus. But man has tried them all and none of them leads anywhere but down.

Christ came to give us the answers to the three enduring problems of sin, sorrow and death. It is Jesus Christ, and He alone, who is also enduring and unchanging, 'the same yesterday, and the today and forever' (Hebrews 13:8). As the hymn writer, Henry F. Lyte, wrote: 'Change and decay in all around I see; O Thou who changest not, abide with me.'

All other things may change, but Christ remains unchangeable. In the restless sea of human passions, Christ stands steadfast and calm, ready to welcome all who will turn to Him and accept the blessings of safety and peace. For we are living in an age of grace, in which God promises that whosoever will may come and receive His Son. But this period of grace will not go on indefinitely. We are even now living on borrowed time.

DAME BERYL GREY, DBE

FORMER PRIMA BALLERINA OF SADLER'S WELLS BALLET AND ARTISTIC
DIRECTOR OF LONDON FESTIVAL BALLET

Dame Beryl was born in London on 11 June 1927. She has appeared in leading roles of many of the world's most famous ballets and even appeared in the world's first three-dimensional ballet film – The Black Swan. *She has danced with some of the world's greatest companies including the Chinese Ballet and the Bolshoi Ballet. Her books include* Red Curtain Up Through the Bamboo Curtain *and* My Favourite Ballet Stories.

Dear Mr Gabay,

THE MEANING OF LIFE.

To me Life has a clear meaning. I believe that on this planet there is a constant battle between good and evil and that we are all being tested. Our souls struggle to return to our Creator. We need to free them from the dominance of our minds in order to allow that spark of Good, which is in us all, to take over. Having been given free will we surely owe it to our Creator to serve him well.

Dame Beryl Grey, DBE

REVD NICKY GUMBELL

FORMER BARRISTER AND ON THE STAFF OF HOLY TRINITY BROMPTON

The Revd Gumbell read law at Cambridge, practised as a barrister, read theology at Oxford and is now ordained and on the staff of Holy Trinity Brompton. He is the leader of the Alpha Course, an introduction to Christianity, at Holy Trinity. He is the author of Why Jesus?, Questions of Life *(winner of the Christian Book of the Year Award 1994/95),* Searching Issues, A Life Worth Living *and* Telling Others. *He is married to Pippa and has three children.*

Men and women were created to live in a relationship with God. Without that relationship there will always be a hunger, an emptiness, a feeling that something is missing. Prince Charles recently spoke of his belief that, for all the advances of science, 'there remains deep in the soul (if I dare use that word), a persistent and unconscious anxiety that something is missing, some ingredient that makes life worth living'.

Bernard Levin, perhaps the greatest columnist of his generation, once wrote an article called 'Life's Great Riddle, and No Time to Find Its Meaning'. In it he spoke of the fact that in spite of his great success as a columnist for over twenty years he feared that he might have 'wasted reality in the chase of a dream'. He wrote:

> To put it bluntly, have I time to discover why I was born before I die? . . . I have not managed to answer the question yet, and however many years I have before me they are certainly not as many as there are behind. There is an obvious danger in leaving it too late . . . why do I have to know why I was born? Because of course, I am unable to believe that it was an accident; and if it wasn't one, it must have been a meaning.

He is not a Christian and wrote recently, 'For the fourteen thousandth time, I am not a Christian.' Yet he seems to be only too aware of the inadequate answers to the meaning of life. He wrote some years earlier:

> Countries like ours are full of people who have all the material comforts they desire, together with non-material blessings as a happy family, and yet lead lives of quiet, and at times noisy, desperation, understanding nothing but the fact that there is a hole inside them

and that however much food and drink they pour into it, however many motor cars and television sets they stuff it with, however many well balanced children and loyal friends they parade around the edges of it . . . it aches.

Some people spend much of their lives seeking something that will give meaning and purpose to life. Leo Tolstoy, author of *War and Peace* and *Anna Karenina*, wrote a book called *A Confession* in 1879, in which he tells the story of his search for meaning and purpose in life. He had rejected Christianity as a child. Moscow and Petersburg, drinking heavily, living promiscuously, gambling and leading a wild life. But it did not satisfy him.

Then he became ambitious for money. He had inherited an estate and made a large amount of money out of his books. Yet that did not satisfy him either. He sought success, fame and importance. These he also achieved. He wrote what the Encyclopaedia Britannica describes as 'one of the two or three greatest novels in world literature'. But he was left asking the question, 'Well fine . . . so what?' To which he had no answer.

Then he became ambitious for his family – to give them the best possible life. He married in 1862 and had a kind, loving wife and thirteen children (which, he says, distracted him from any search for the overall meaning of life!). He had achieved all his ambitions and was surrounded by what appeared to be complete happiness. And yet one question brought him to the verge of suicide: 'Is there any meaning in life which will not be annihilated by the inevitability of death which awaits me?'

He searched for the answer in every field of science and philosophy. The only answer he could find to the question 'Why do I live?' was that in the infinity of space and the infinity of time infinitely small particles mutate with infinite complexity.

As he looked around at his contemporaries he saw that people were not facing up to the first order questions of life. ('Where did I come from?', 'Where am I heading?', 'Who am I?', 'What is life about?') Eventually he found that the peasant people of Russia had been able to answer these questions through their Christian faith and he came to realise that only in Jesus Christ do we find the answer.

Over a hundred years later nothing has changed. Freddie Mercury the lead singer of the rock group Queen, who died at the end of 1991, wrote in one of his last songs, 'Does anybody know what we are living for?' In spite of the fact that he had amassed a huge fortune and had attracted thousands of fans, he admitted in an interview shortly before his death that he was desperately lonely. He said, 'You can have everything in the world and still be the loneliest man, and that is the most bitter type of loneliness. Success has brought me world idolisation and millions of pounds, but it has prevented me from having the one thing we all need – a loving ongoing relationship.'

He was right to speak of an 'ongoing relationship' as the one thing we all need. Yet no human relationship will satisfy entirely. Nor can it be completely ongoing. There always remains something missing. That is because we are created to live in a relationship with God. Jesus said, 'I am the way.' He is the only one who can bring us into the relationship with God that goes on into eternity.

When I was a child our family had an old black and white television set. We could never get a very good picture; it was always fuzzy and used to go into lines. We were quite happy with it since we did not know anything different. One day we discovered that it needed an outside aerial! Suddenly we found that we could get clear and distinct pictures. Our enjoyment was transformed. Life without a relationship with God through Jesus Christ is like the television without the aerial. Some people seem quite happy, because they don't realise that there is something better. Once we have experienced a relationship with God the purpose and meaning of life should become clear. We see things that we have never seen, and it would be foolish to want to return to the old life. We understand why we were made.

H

Life's a piece in bloom, Death goes dogging everywhere; she's the tenant of the room, he's the ruffian on the stair.

WILLIAM ERNEST HENLEY

Money is life to us wretched mortals.

HESIOD

Do not take life too seriously; you will never get out of it alive.

ELBERT HUBBARD

We are a part of the eternities and have a part to play in their orchestrated symphonic movements.

E. G. HIRSCH

DR LESLIE HAMILTON, MD, FRCP

CONSULTANT PAEDIATRIC CARDIAC SURGEON

In 1993 Dr Hamilton was one of only 70 doctors recommended by a panel of over 50 senior consultants and professors as a leading specialist they would personally turn to for treatment. (Another two, Professor Adrian Harris and Professor Michael Hull are also included in this book.) Dr Hamilton specialises in children's heart transplants at the Freeman Hospital in Newcastle-upon-Tyne.

The Meaning of Life . . . a question addressed by philosophers over the centuries and one which has perplexed each succeeding generation. As a surgeon I have to make decisions – ultimately to cut or not to cut. Thus, I have to approach problems in clear terms – no grey areas are allowed or I would never make any decisions. Therefore, in answering the question as to the meaning of life, or to phrase it another way, why are we here?, it would seem to me that I have two choices: either we evolved randomly from a primeval 'soup' or we were created. If the former, I can see no logical basis for any meaning of life and as individuals we might as well be completely self-centred – there would be no logical basis for caring and we are thus no different from any other members of the animal world. If the latter, what is our relationship with the creator?

Philosophically, therefore, I am a Christian. I believe that we were created by God, who gave us our own free will – as human beings we have chosen to distance ourselves from God and this to me explains the evil in society and the selfishness evident in human relationships. However, God provided an opportunity to restore the original relationship between ourselves and God by sending his son, Jesus Christ, who through his death and resurrection became a mediator between us. For me this is the rational answer to the question of why we are here. One measure of mankind's humanity is surely how humanely people treat one another. To paraphrase: I care, therefore, I am (and if I do not care I am not).

PROFESSOR ADRIAN L. HARRIS

PROFESSOR OF ONCOLOGY

Adrian Harris is the director of the Imperial Cancer Research Fund Clinical Oncology Unit and Molecular Oncology laboratories at the Institute of Molecular Medicine in Oxford. He is particularly interested in the treatment of common solid cancers and developing new treatment approaches, involving the inhibition of angiogenesis and gene therapy.

Life has no meaning other than that which man chooses to give it. Human life evolved on this planet over the time period of a thousand million years or longer, and it is only in the last ten centuries that highly organised societies have developed. Humans therefore have entered a new phase of evolution involving social evolution, and the present diversity of life styles and beliefs demonstrates fertility of the human mind and that there is no single correct answer.

Man now however can control his environment, whereas in the past he merely reacted to it. Thus not only in social but in environmental and physical matters man has far greater control over his evolution than was ever possible previously. However, life has to have a value in order to have a meaning – without value there is no meaning.

Those societies that have the most successful survival outcomes are those that are following rules or guidelines of behaviour that maximise the value of life. Thus societies that value human life the most will do the most to preserve life and improve the quality of life. Those societies with the best life expectancy, lowest rate of mortality and greatest proportion of children reaching maturity in a healthy state are using guidelines that provide a meaning to life.

It is clear that human beings need to be valued by other human beings to feel they have a useful role in society. It is also apparent that human beings have a vast repertoire of creative abilities and that during their lives they should have the maximum chances to utilise and develop these skills.

If we assume that our emotions and social interactions also underwent evolution and those that were best for survival are the ones that have been retained, then it is clear that working together as groups rather than as isolated individuals has been of benefit. The drive for individual excellence or achievement is one meaning to life, but can only be achieved in the context of team effort. As a greater variety of social structures are tried it will become increasingly clear what provides the best quality of life and life expectancy.

The value of human life is maximising the contribution one can make to the society in which one lives, which should in return maximise contribution to the individual, and it is noteworthy that societies that have given the most individual freedom in intellectual pursuit are also the ones that have made the greatest contributions to science, medicine and improving life expectancy in the last 100 years. Evolution shows us that stagnation eventually leads to the death of the species, and it is only through vitality, innovation, exploration and development that species will survive.

Man has an unprecedented opportunity of both controlling his future and enhancing all aspects of life. It is apparent in dealing with patients that value by others and having others to value, optimising one's own effort and enjoying what life has to offer, and contributing to the common good are major man-generated meanings of life. Good quality of life provides a purpose in itself, but if one has a fatal illness/severe deprivation this does not apply and other meanings are sought, e.g. preparation for an afterlife, punishment by illness. It is human nature to look for meanings and explanation; which is why the human race has been successful.

Life has evolved in much more severe circumstances than any environmental damage that man has so far produced, and will continue to be able to evolve whatever the environmental circumstances. With the development of consciousness man can ask questions that other species never could. The meaning of life is a man-made question and the answer is made by man. If man holds life to be of little value or no value, the societies that have that approach ultimately will fail and will never be able to maximise on the potential of the human brain and intellect, or provide happiness to most people.

SIR JOHN HARVEY-JONES, Kt, MBE

BUSINESS EXECUTIVE

Sir John was born on 16 April 1924. He served with the Royal Navy, 1937–56, specialising in submarines, and later worked with National Intelligence. He joined ICI as a work study officer in 1936, was appointed technical director in 1967 and held the office of chairman between 1982 and 1987. He is currently the chairman of Parallax Enterprises. In 1991 he was named British Businessman of the Year.

SIR JOHN HARVEY-JONES MBE
CHAIRMAN

PARALLAX ENTERPRISES LTD.
P.O. BQX 18
ROSS-ON-WYE
HEREFORDSHIRE HR9 7TL
VAT No. 467 8375 92

TEL: 0989 780430
FAX No. 0989 780427

7th June, 1994

Dear Jonathan

Thank you for your letter of the 20th May.

I believe that the meaning of life is to attempt to leave the world and society a little better than it was when one was born.

All of us stand in a position of stewardship not only for our friends, colleagues and associates but for the environment and the world as a whole, including the animal kingdom. At minimum our aim should be to ensure that things are not made any worse. I believe a satisfactory life involves actively trying to make things better.

Yours sincerely

[signature]

Directors: Sir John Harvey-Jones (Chairman), Gabrielle Harvey-Jones (Company Secretary), F.W.B. Atcheson, Lady Harvey-Jones
Company Registered in England & Wales - Number 2052815. Registered Office: 66 Queen Square, Bristol, BS1 4JP. VAT No. 467 8375 92

PROFESSOR STEPHEN HAWKING, CH, CBE, PhD, FRS

PROFESSOR OF MATHEMATICS, COSMOLOGIST AND THEORETICAL PHYSICIST

Professor Hawking was born on 8 January 1942. He has been confined to a wheelchair for over twenty years by a motor neurone disease. He has several degrees and has won various awards including the William Hopkins Prize and the Wolf Prize. His books include A Brief History of Time, Superspace *and* Supergravity.

We find ourselves in a bewildering world. We want to make sense of what we see around us and to ask: What is the nature of the universe? What is our place in it and where did it and we come from? Why is it the way it is?

To try to answer these questions we adopt some 'world picture'. Just as an infinite tower of tortoises supporting the flat earth is such a picture, so is the theory of superstrings. Both are theories of the universe, though the latter is much more mathematical and precise than the former. Both theories lack observational evidence: no one has ever seen a giant tortoise with the earth on its back, but then, no one has seen a superstring either. However, the tortoise theory fails to be a good scientific theory because it predicts that people should be able to fall off the edge of the world. This has not been found to agree with experience, unless that turns out to be the explanation for the people who are supposed to have disappeared in the Bermuda Triangle!

The earliest theoretical attempts to describe and explain the universe involved the idea that events and natural phenomena were controlled by spirits with human emotions who acted in a very humanlike and unpredictable manner. These spirits inhabited natural objects, like rivers and mountains, including celestial bodies, like the sun and moon. They had to be placated and their favours sought in order to ensure the fertility of the soil and the rotation of the seasons. Gradually, however, it must have been noticed that there were certain regularities: the sun always rose in the east and set in the west, whether or not a sacrifice had been made to the sun god. Further, the sun, the moon and the planets followed precise paths across the sky that could be predicted in advance with considerable accuracy. The sun and the moon might still be gods, but they were gods who obeyed strict laws, apparently without any options, if one discounts stories like that of the sun stopping for Joshua.

At first, these regularities and laws were obvious only in astronomy and a few other situations. However, as civilisation developed, and particularly in the last 300 years, more and more regularities and laws were discovered. The success of these laws led Laplace at the beginning of the nineteenth century to postulate scientific determinism. That is, he suggested that these would be a set of laws that would determine the evolution of the universe precisely, given its configuration at one time.

Laplace's determinism was incomplete in two ways. It did not say how the laws would be chosen and it did not specify the initial configuration of the universe. These were left to God. God would choose how the universe began and what laws would be obeyed, but he would intervene in the universe once it had started. In effect, God was confined to the areas that nineteenth-century science did not understand.

We now know that Laplace's hopes of determinism cannot be realised, at least in the terms he had in mind. The uncertainty principle of quantum mechanics implies that certain pairs of quantities, such as the position and velocity of a particle, cannot both be predicted with complete accuracy.

Quantum mechanics deals with this situation via a class of quantum theories in which particles don't have well-defined positions and velocities but are represented by a wave. The quantum theories are deterministic in the sense that they give laws for the evolution of the wave with time. Thus if one knows the wave at one time, one can calculate it at any other time. The unpredictable, random element comes in only when we try to interpret the wave in terms of the positions and velocities of particles. But maybe that is our mistake: maybe there are no particle positions and velocities, but only waves. It is just that we try to fit the waves to our preconceived ideas of positions and velocities. The resulting mis-match is the cause of apparent unpredictability.

In effect, we have redefined the task of science to be the discovery of laws that will enable us to predict events up to the limits set by the uncertainty principle. The question remains, however: How or why were the laws and the initial state of the universe chosen?

I give special prominence to the laws that govern gravity, because it is gravity that shapes the large-scale structure of the universe, even though it is the weakest of the four categories of forces. The laws of gravity were compatible with the view held until quite recently that the universe is changing in time: that fact that gravity is always attractive implies that the universe must be either expanding or contracting. According to the general theory of relativity, there must have been a rate of infinite density in the past, the big bang, which would have been an effective beginning of time. Similarly, if the whole universe recollapsed, there must be another state of infinite density in the future, the big crunch, which would be an end of time. Even if the whole universe did not recollapse, there would be singularities in any localised regions that collapsed to form black holes.

These singularities would be an end of time for anyone who fell into the black hole. At the big bang and other singularities, all the laws would have broken down, so God would still have had complete freedom to choose what happened and how the universe began.

When we combine quantum mechanics with general relativity, there seems to be a new possibility that did not arise before: that space and time together might form a finite, four dimensional space without singularities or boundaries, like the surface of the earth but with more dimensions. It seems that this idea could explain many of the observed features of the universe, such as its large scale uniformity and also the smaller scale departures from homogeneity, like galaxies, stars, and even human beings. It could even account for the arrow of time that we observe. But if the universe is completely self-contained, with no singularities or boundaries, and completely described by a unified theory, that has profound implications for the role of God as Creator.

Einstein once asked the question: 'How much choice did God have in constructing the universe?' If the no boundary proposal is correct, he had no freedom at all to choose initial conditions. He would, of course, still have had the freedom to choose the laws that the universe obeyed. This however may not really have been all that much of a choice; there may well be only one, or a small number, of complete unified theories, such as the heterotic string theory, that are self-consistent and allow the existence of structures as complicated as human beings who can investigate the laws of the universe and ask about the nature of God.

Even if there is only one possible unified theory, it is just a set of rules and equations. What is it that breathes fire into the equations and makes a universe for them to describe? The usual approach of science of constructing a mathematical model cannot answer the questions of why there should be a universe for the model to describe. Why does the universe go to all the bother of existing? Is the unified theory so compelling that it brings about its own existence? Or does it need a creator, and, if so, does he have any other effect on the universe? And who created him?

Up to now, most scientists have been too occupied with the development of new theories that describe what the universe is to ask the question why. On the other hand, the people whose business is to ask why, the philosophers, have not been able to keep up with the advance of scientific theories. In the eighteenth century, philosophers considered the whole human knowledge, including science, to be their field and discussed questions such as: Did the universe have a beginning? However, in the nineteenth and twentieth centuries, science became too technical and mathematical for the philosophers, or anyone else except a few specialists.

Philosophers reduce the scope of their inquiries so much that Wittgenstein, the most famous philosopher of the century, said, 'The sole remaining task for philosophy is the analysis of language.' What a comedown from the great tradition of philosophy from Aristotle to Kant!

However, if we do discover a complete theory, it should in time be understandable in broad principle by everyone, not just a few scientists. Then we shall all, philosophers, scientists, and just ordinary people, be able to take part in the discussion of the question of why it is that we and the universe exist. If we find the answer to that, it would be the ultimate triumph of human reason – for then we would know the mind of God.

From *A Brief History of Time* by Stephen Hawking. Reprinted by permission of Bantam Press Limited.

NIGEL HAWTHORNE, CBE

ACTOR

Nigel was born in Coventry on 5 April 1929. He was educated in South Africa and entered the theatre professionally in 1950. His stage work includes Privates on Parade *and* The Madness of George III *and he has appeared in* The Knowledge, Yes Minister *and* Yes Prime Minister *on television. Most recently he has starred in* The Madness of King George, *which was nominated for an Academy Award.*

13th May 1994

Dear Mr Gabay,

I have your letter saying that you are contacting a wide range of people in the hope that they will be able to answer your question "What is the meaning of Life?".

It occurs to me that you will find the meaning of life not from other people's opinions but from your own experience.

Yours sincerely,

NIGEL HAWTHORNE

73

SIR MICHAEL HORDEN, Kt, CBE

ACTOR

Sir Michael was born on 3 October 1911. He was educated at Brighton College and began acting as an amateur at St Pancras People's Theatre. Giving up a life in business to pursue a career as an actor, his natural talents earned him the reputation as being one of England's finest character players. Tragically, Sir Michael died just before the publication of this book. This makes his contribution particularly poignant as these are probably his last published words.

May 13 '94

Dear Mr Gabay

I'm sorry but I see, at the end of mine, no meaning to life but to "fade into the light of common day"

Michael Horden

MOST REVD TREVOR HUDDLESTON, CR, DD

CHAIRMAN OF THE INTERNATIONAL DEFENCE AND AIR FUND FOR SOUTH AFRICA

The Revd Huddleston was educated in Oxford. He became Bishop of Masai and Mauritius and Archbishop of the Indian Ocean. He held the post of President of the Anti-Apartheid Movement from 1981 to 1994 and has also been on the National Peace Council.

In the words of the Prophet Micah the answer is 'to do justly, to love mercy and to walk humbly with your God'. This is an exact answer because it clearly joins good intention with action. If we are to be fulfilled in life we must work for a just society, a compassionate society and a God-centred society.

PROFESSOR MICHAEL HULL, MD, FRCOG

PROFESSOR OF REPRODUCTIVE MEDICINE AND SURGERY

Professor Hull was born in 1939 and is a consultant obstetrician and gynaecologist. He specialises in reproductive endocrinology and all aspects of both male and female infertility and leads a clinical and laboratory research team exploring hormonal factors affecting health and egg, sperm and fertilisation factors affecting fertility.

Life is. It has no meaning, but is the means of experience. At its most basic it is sensibility. That is inescapable, but may be enjoyed or hurtful, and prevented or improved by intelligent motive power. Sympathy, and regard for others' comfort – and at a higher level, their happiness – require refined intelligence. To believe in the ultimate human doctrine of 'love thy neighbour' doesn't need a god. It does, however, require conditioned experience. The best conditioning is love. Life may have no logical meaning but at its best it is love and happiness.

Lack of parental love must be the most damaging experience. If life were to have any purposeful meaning, one key would have to be the fostering of love in children. Lack of children to love robs life of its greatest source of happiness and purpose.

REVD JOSEPH FRANCIS HUMBLE

RETIRED ANGLICAN PRIEST

The Revd Joseph was born on 9 November 1924 in Doncaster, South York-shire. He studied at Oxford University and has held various ecclesiastic positions including vicar of a mining parish in South Yorkshire and vicar of a large parish in Leamington. He has also worked overseas with The Missions to Seamen. Revd Joseph was diagnosed as being HIV positive in 1986. Today he still works as an assistant priest at St Mark's, Regents Park, London and says, 'I feel fine.'

I find this a puzzling phrase. In fact I don't know what it means. So may I try and answer the question, 'What is the purpose of life?'

Whatever I am doing I try to ask myself the question, 'What is my aim?' 'Why am I doing what I am doing?' and I ask that question of other people too.

When I was first diagnosed HIV positive, I was devastated. Later I took the decision to leave no stone unturned to be well. The result of that was that I was doing all kinds of things which were not very easy or pleasant. And I asked myself, 'Is it worth it?' While I was asking myself this question I came across a little book by Monica Furlong describing the work of the Anglican centre of spiritual healing at Burswood. Someone there had asked himself the same question. He came up with the answer, 'To glorify God.'

I found that, and do find it, a satisfying motive for taking the trouble to be well.

Of course this phrase is the part of the answer given by the Anglican shorter catechism to the question, 'What is the chief end of man?'. The answer is, 'To glorify God and enjoy Him for ever.'

The next question after that is, 'How?'

Each person must find the answer to that for himself.

I have dared to ask the question about aims of Jesus Christ Himself. He gives the answer in Chapter 10 of St John's Gospel, verse 10: 'I have come that you should have life, and have it to the full.'

It seems to me that the vocation of every Christian is to try to do the same for those among whom he lives.

TONY HUSBAND

CARTOONIST

Tony was born in 1948. He has been a full-time cartoonist for eight years and his work has appeared in the Daily Star, Private Eye, Punch, The Sunday Times, Men Only, Playboy, Oldie *and many more publications. He is a co-writer of the award-winning children's television programme,* Round the Bend, *and has won many awards including Joke Cartoonist of the Year and Strip Cartoonist of the Year.*

You Do the Hokey Cokey and you turn around thats what its all about.

I, J

It is better to die on your feet than live on your knees.

EUGÈNE IONESCO

Believe that life is worth living and your belief will help create the fact.

WILLIAM JAMES

Man was created to learn wisdom.

JOB

Life is a steady walk with a hidden precipice at the end.

LAMBERT JEFFRIES

Life is a progress from want to want, not from enjoyment to enjoyment.

SAMUEL JOHNSON

GLENDA JACKSON, CBE

POLITICIAN AND ACTRESS

Glenda was born in Birkenhead on 9 May 1936. She joined the Royal Shakespeare Company in 1963. Her stage appearances include All Kinds of Men, The Jew of Malta, *and* The White Devil *and she has starred in films such as* This Sporting Life, A Touch of Class *and* The Rainbow. *She has been MP (Lab) for Hampstead and Highgate since 1992.*

GLENDA JACKSON, M.P.

HOUSE OF COMMONS
LONDON SW1A 0AA
071-219 4008

Mr Jonathan Gabay,
32 Springfield Gardens,
London NW9 ORS.   June 1994

Dear Mr Gabay,

Thank you for your letter.

In reply to your request for a
quotation I think the words of
E. M. Forster "Only connect" would
do very well.

Good luck with your project - I hope
your book is very successful.

Best wishes,

                    Yours sincerely,

                    Glenda Jackson.

BARON IMMANUEL JAKOBOVITZ

FORMER CHIEF RABBI OF THE UNITED HEBREW CONGREGATIONS OF THE BRITISH
COMMONWEALTH OF NATIONS

Rabbi Jakobovitz was born on 8 February 1921 and he was educated in London. His first ministry was at Brondesbury Synagogue and he became Chief Rabbi of Ireland as well as Rabbi of 5th Avenue Synagogue in New York. His prizes include the Templeton Prize for Progress in Religion and he has written a number of books including Jewish Law Faces Modern Problems *and the centenary edition of the* Authorised Daily Prayer Book.

Dear Mr Gabay,

The meaning of life, as I understand it, is to fulfil the purpose for which we were created.

Sincerely yours,
Jakobovitz

K, L

A man's life worth is a continual allegory, and very few can see the mystery of his life – a life like the scriptures, figurative – which some people can no more make out than they can the Hebrew bible. Lord Byron cuts a figure – but he is not figurative – Shakespeare led a life of allegory: his works are the comments on it.

JOHN KEATS

life is what happens to you while you're busy making other plans.

JOHN LENNON

Life is like a sewer. What you get out of it depends on what you put into it.

TOM LEHRER

Life is something to do when you can't get to sleep.

FRAN LEBOWITZ

PROFESSOR EPHRAIM KATZIR, PhD EMERITUS

PROFESSOR AT WEIZMANN INSTITUTE, FORMERLY PRESIDENT, STATE OF ISRAEL

Ephraim was born in Kiev, Ukraine on 16 May 1916. He moved with his parents to Israel in 1922. He is professor emeritus at the Tel Aviv University and professor at Weizmann Institute of Science. He has won several international and national awards and was the President of the World ORT Union, and the fourth President of the State of Israel.

I speak as a scientist and a Jew.

Many anthropologists agree that the human mind sets the humans species apart from the rest of the natural world. Some say being human means that we possess culture; and indeed it is our capacity for culture, that distinctive expression of our artificial gene, which makes us human.

Jews are born into a cultural heritage. The supreme importance of human life is explicit in the Torah, and resounds throughout the Jewish literature. 'If one destroys a life, it is as though one has destroyed the world, while if one saves a life, it is as though one has saved the world.' Jews who perished at Nazi hands believed to the end in the liberating power of life. They would proclaim in the ghettos and in the concentration camps: 'This is the time for kiddush Ha-chaim (the sanctification of life), not for kiddush Hashem (martyrdom).'

Jews have a special regard for children and belief in a better future. It is here, and not in any life hereafter, that things will improve – if not for us at least for our children, certainly for our children's children. So the chain of life goes on. We must nurture the coming generation for it is they who will inherit a better future.

The coming together of scientific thought and religious belief is wonderfully expressed by Teilhard de Chardin. 'Man is not the centre of the Universe, as we naively believed in the past, but something much more beautiful – man is the ascending arrow of the great biological synthesis of life: man is the best born, the keenest, the most complex, the most subtle of the successive layers of life, into his hands are entrusted the future of the coming generations, of all living creatures, and even of our planet itself.'

In the stirring words of Deuteronomy – 'I have set before you life and death, the blessing and the curse; therefore choose life, that both thou and thy seed may live.'

SIR LUDOVIC KENNEDY, Kt

JOURNALIST

Sir Ludovic was born on 3 November 1919. He was educated at Eton and Christ Church, Oxford. He has been a lecturer, newspaper director, television presenter and columnist. His awards include the Richard Dimbleby BAFTA Award and the First Class Order of Ment, Federal Republic of Germany. TV work includes This Week, Panorama *and* Face the Press. The Trial of Stephen Ward *and* Euthanasia: The Good Death *are just two of a number of publications.*

4th October 1994

Dear Mr Gabay

There is no meaning of life other than what individuals care to give to it.

Yours sincerely

Sir Ludovic Kennedy

GRAHAM KENTFIELD

CHIEF OF THE BANKING DEPARTMENT AND CHIEF CASHIER OF THE BANK OF
ENGLAND

Graham was born on 3 September 1940. He entered the Bank of England in 1963 and was deputy chief of the banking department and deputy chief cashier between 1985 and 1991. You can see his signature on every current bank note in England (check it for yourself!).

G E A Kentfield
Chief of the Banking Department
and Chief Cashier
071-601 4361

BANK OF ENGLAND
LONDON EC2R 8AH

17 February 1994

Dear Mr Gabay

Thank you for your letter of 8 February. I am flattered that you think I come within the category of "highly-respected national and international leading figures and admired personalities", but I fear that I cannot answer your question in non-religious terms. As a committed member of the Church of England, I am clear that the meaning of life can only properly be understood in the context of man's relationship to God. I commend to you St John's Gospel as a better answer to your question than any which I could devise.

Yours sincerely

G E A Kentfield.

THE RT HON. NEIL KINNOCK

EUROPEAN TRANSPORT COMMISSIONER

Neil was born on 28 March 1942 and entered national politics in 1970. He was PPS to the Secretary of State for Employment from 1974 to 1975 and has been a member of the National Executive of the Labour Party since 1978. He was the principal opposition front bench spokesman on education from 1979 to 1983 and leader of the Labour Party between 1983 and 1992. He is currently European Transport Commissioner. His publications include Wales and the Common Market *and* Making Our Way – Investing in Britain's Future.

For a human being; life must be given meaning by relating to others – helping others, being helped by others, giving and taking knowledge, sympathy, fun – all the things that make existence worthwhile. *Mutuality* is the essence of life.

GLENYS KINNOCK, MEP

Glenys was born on 7 July 1944. She is married to The Rt Hon. Neil Kinnock. Before entering politics she was a secondary and primary school teacher. In addition to her work as an MEP she has been on the board of UNICEF. Her books include Eritrea: Images of War and Peace *and* Namibia – Birth of a Nation.

The meaning of life for me is impossible to define or describe because at different times my priorities change. However, encapsulated, the greatest joy has been having a happy marriage based on real friendship and trust and having two wonderful children who have made us both very proud.

CHRISTOPHER LEE

ACTOR, AUTHOR AND DIRECTOR

Christopher was born on 27 May 1922. He entered the film industry in 1947 and has appeared in over 200 motion pictures including Moulin Rouge, A Tale of Two Cities, The Man with the Golden Gun *and* The Hound of the Baskervilles. *His most famous role has been Dracula. His publications include* Christopher Lee's Treasury of Terror, Christopher Lee's Archives of Evil *and* Tall, Dark and Gruesome *(autobiography).*

Dear Mr Gabay,

What is the meaning of life? I refer you to Polonius's words from *Hamlet* – 'This above all; to thine own self be true.'

Yours sincerely,
Christopher Lee

LEE TENG-HUI, PhD

PRESIDENT OF THE REPUBLIC OF CHINA (TAIWAN)

President Teng-Hui was born on 15 January 1923 in Tamsui. He was educated in Japan and America. He spent his early career as an assistant professor at Taiwan University as well as being professor of economics and a research fellow. Following a career in banking he moved over to political life. He has held various posts such as Minister of State and Mayor of Taipei. He became President of the Republic of China (Taiwan) in 1988.

府統總國民華中

OFFICE OF THE PRESIDENT OF THE REPUBLIC OF CHINA

October 14, 1994

Dear Mr. Gabay:

I am writing to acknowledge receipt of your letter dated September 11, 1994, on behalf of President Lee Teng-hui.

The President fully endorses your idea of publishing a book on the meaning of life to raise funds for the British Red Cross in its international humanitarian relief efforts. He is therefore delighted to share with you some of his thoughts about life, quoted from his book <u>Love and Faith</u>, as follows:

"Our lives will be made richer and more meaningful through loving others and pursuing noble ideals and beliefs."

"People from different walks of life have different ideals. Politicians want to win more welfare for the people. Scientists want to make new discoveries. Educators want to cultivate more talent. Artists and writers want to create more inspirational and thought-provoking works. The ideals are different, but their desire to contribute to society and the nation is consistent."

"In sacrificing ourselves and abandoning our 'self,' our aim is not to benefit ourselves but to show concern and do good for others."

I am sending you herewith a copy of <u>Love and Faith</u> for your reference. And, in quoting President Lee, please refer to him as President of the Republic of China.

BERNARD LEVIN, CBE

JOURNALIST AND AUTHOR

Bernard was born on 19 August 1928. He was educated at the University of London where he received a BSc in economics. He has written for many newspapers and magazines in Britain and abroad including The Times, The Sunday Times, Observer, Manchester Guardian, Spectator, Daily Express, Daily Mail, Newsweek *and* International Herald Tribune. *Bernard has also written and broadcast for radio and television. His contribution is an article he wrote entitled 'Life's Great Riddle, and No Time to Find its Meaning', first published on 1 January 1991 in* The Times.

Considering the number of times I have said that if I were minded to make away with myself I would certainly do it on New Year's Eve, I think my readers would be well advised to turn this page for a moment, to see if my obituary is on the next verso. No? Then I shall continue.

'Another year! – another deadly blow,' said Wordsworth, adding, 'And we are left, or shall be left, alone'. Too many of my friends and acquaintances, heedless of my exhortations, have taken to dying, choosing 1990 to do it in; there was one horrendous visitation which obliged me to deliver two memorial addresses in a week.

I am not normally a gloomy fellow; I flatter myself that I can still set the table on a roar. But the end of a year is inevitably a measuring; someone rang me up a few weeks ago to ask if I would be interviewed under the heading 'My health and I' (that's nothing where lunacy is concerned – another interview was requested for, so help me, a series called 'My image and I'), and after I had declined, which was immediately, and giggled a bit, which was soon after, it occurred to me that 1990 had included not only fallen arches (well, one fallen arch) but about 240 yards of computer print-out on the couch of a most diligent cardiologist searching for the visible traces of an irregular heart-beat which he had happened upon auscultationally. (Don't be alarmed; I have had an irregular heartbeat since I was born, and it has not troubled me. He was only seeking the evidence and providing assurance.)

There are other aspects of mortality. I used to have an exceptional memory; indeed it was so exceptional that it was truly freakish. But there was a trap in it, which I never spotted; because I could retrieve at will and with the greatest exactitude matter many years or even decades old, I kept no files, no cuttings, no sources, nothing. So perfect was my recall that for years I did not even keep an address-book, knowing that the details required were ready to be produced from the appropriate synapse. Now, the familiar stigmata of fading memory can be seen in an inability to remember people's names, for instance, or a doubt as to whether I have already sent that letter; this, as I say, is a familiar experience as the years advance, but for me the pain is greater than for most, because I have to measure the natural level of failing memory against the unnatural level of my former success.

I had better face the truth; I am never going to read Motley's *The Rise of the Dutch Republic*. It has been sitting on my shelves since I was a schoolboy, and if you add up the words in all the promises I have made to take it down one day and read it, you would probably find that they come to more than there are words in the accusing volume. (The trouble is that it sits – I have no idea why – next to the Rawlinson version of Herodotus, and every time I think I will break my duck at last, my fingers stray to my old friend.)

The point of all this is not just that I am never going to read Motley; it is that I have finally admitted as much, and you wouldn't believe the relief I felt when the guilt lifted. I got over my Proust-guilt long ago, I am happy to say, and powerful reinforcement for my conclusion that the first 70 pages of *Swanns Way* are all that is necessary was provided very recently in the *TLS*, where I found a review of the *eighteenth* volume of Proust's letters. This covered 1918, and assuming that the epistolary torrent comes at the rate of one splash a year, there must be three more to come, since Proust died in 1921 (even he, I take it, cannot write letters posthumously); it gives me a warm feeling to know with the utmost certainty that, having decided not to read the *Recherche* itself, I am certainly not, *a fortiori*, going to read the letters.

I suppose I am clearing the decks; Motley is a very good symbol of the necessity of knowing what we cannot do. Once, we thought we could do anything, and you would be amazed at the length of time it took to make me understand that that is a fallacy; I am by no means the worst – some go on to the end of their lives never knowing that they have wasted reality in the chase of a dream. Yet even I cannot gainsay that 'coming to terms' is one of the most depressing phrases ever coined. I never could run a mile in four minutes, so it does not distress me that I can't now; but I could once recite without faltering the whole of *Lepanto*, and it distresses me beyond measure to find that I can no longer do so.

But it is worse even than that. The other day, a most cheering announcement was made: it seems that Birmingham is going to be pulled down. Unfortunately, it is going to be put up again, but that cannot be helped. The point, where I was concerned, was that the key date of the rebuilding is to be 1995. I repeat: I am not given to gloom, let alone general pessimism, but the thought came into my head unbidden, and bid it leave as I might, it stayed there, thumbing its nose at me. Would I see the end of Birmingham's reincarnation? (I have no wish to do so, of course, because whatever they put in its place will be at least as hideous as what is to be demolished, but I wouldn't want to miss it for *that* reason.)

And how about this? In a couple of weeks' time I shall celebrate (if that is the word, and the way I feel at the moment it certainly is not) the 20th anniversary of the first column I wrote for *The Times*. William Rees-Mogg, who had not long since become the editor, invited me to join the paper, and I did so at the beginning of 1970 (also the year my first book was published). The *Times* office was then still at Printing House Square, and space was by no means easy to come by (it is a damned sight more difficult at Wapping, I can tell you – or even if I can't, my colleagues can and will), and I parked myself in his outer office and got down to work. He had initially asked me to write one column a week, but a year or so later he asked me to do two, and later on raised it, so help me, to three. (That nearly killed me – so nearly, indeed, that I eventually took an immense sabbatical, well over a year long, and came back determined never again to write more than once a week; you see how my promise was kept.)

I have been fortunate beyond most journalists in my relations with *Times* editors; the present one is the fifth I have worked with, and never a cross word. Wailings and moanings, yes; Rees-Mogg's screams of horror, as he contemplated yet another couple of thousand words of the most extravagant libel, could be heard on the other side of the Thames.

Mind you, I was in at the birth of one of the most magnificent phrases an editor ever finished a leader with. He came out of his room one day, put a galley-proof on my desk, and said, 'Can I really print that?' I looked at it, and replied, 'If you *don't* print it, I will never speak to you again.' It was, of course, the famous peroration: 'Anyway, George Brown drunk is a better man than Harold Wilson sober.'

Twenty years a columnist! I am sure that I do not hold the record, but I would be interested to know who does. Of course, there have been journalistic careers lasting 50 years or more, but the very existence of the modern columnist is very recent as newspapers go; certainly I was the first of these on *The Times*. To think that I have been giving my opinion – which is the rough and ready definition of the breed – year in and year out for two decades, chills my blood, which has anyway cooled quite enough for my liking with the passing of time. I hope – well, I *suppose* – that unless I go completely gaga I shall never run out of opinions to express; I have never yet sat down to write a column without having at least three suitable subjects in mind, and that's a comfort, I can tell you.

Yes, but what about the rest of it? To put it bluntly: have I time to discover why I was born before I die? Silly question: the knowledge can come, complete and rounded, in the twinkling of an eye (an assurance first given to the Corinthians), and I am no more barred from the discovery than anyone else. Nevertheless, I have to admit that I have not managed to answer the question yet, and however many years I have before me they are certainly not as many as there are behind. There is an obvious danger in leaving it too late, but there is a still more intriguing question in this exploration: why do I *have* to know why I was born?

Because, of course, I am unable to believe that it was an accident; and if it wasn't one, it must have a meaning, from which follows the truth that with sufficient diligence and determination a meaning can always be understood. Villon, whom I read more and more now, summed up the desperation of the unanswered question:

Prince, je congnois tout en somme,
Je congnois coulourez et blesmes,
Je congnois Mort qui tout consomme,
Je congnois tout, fors que moy mesmes.

No, I cannot translate it; it is untranslatable, and always will be. I have 17 versions on my shelves, including German and Italian ones, and they are *all* perfectly dreadful. Even transliterating Villon into modern French destroys it. Shut up and read him in the original until you understand.

'Until you understand'; must we be in some other-world corner with a dunce's cap on, until our darkness is lightened? No, it cannot be like that; nothing is given, but everything is there to seek. Nor am I convinced that when the ultimate question is put to me, and I reply 'Well, I was a frightfully good columnist for at least twenty years', it will be judged sufficient. True, this is the first day of Mozart's year, and if we listen carefully until New Year's Eve 1991 we can get some tips; but even they will be only tips on how to seek the answer, not the answer itself.

'Be still, then, and know that I am God.' But what about poor devils like me, who suffer so badly from St Vitus's dance that we cannot be still? Perhaps, after all, I did take the rat-poison as the clocks chimed midnight; have another peek at the obits, would you? But stay: Surely such dreadful and momentous news would be on the front page. Turn back!

M

This world is like a lobby before the world to come; prepare yourself in the lobby that you may enter into the hall.

RABBI JACOBS (MISHNAH)

The Utopian way of life provides not only the happiest basis for a civilised community, but also one which, in all human probability will last for ever.

THOMAS MORE

Hasten to do good before you are overtaken by perplexing adversity, corrupting prosperity, disabling disease, babbling dotage and sudden death.

THE PROPHET MUHAMMAD

BARON JAMES MACKAY OF CLASHFERN

LORD CHANCELLOR OF ENGLAND

The Lord Chancellor was born in Sutherland in 1927. He was called to the Bar in 1955 and ten years later was made a QC, specialising in tax law. He was made Lord Advocate for Scotland and a life peer by Margaret Thatcher in 1979. He became Lord Chancellor in 1987.

Answering the question – what is the meaning of life – is something that some of the most famous philosophers and divines throughout the history of the world have spent much of their time attempting to answer. I cannot hope to match the insights that they have provided but, as a Christian, I draw my inspiration from the Bible and the teachings of Jesus Christ.

SIR IAN McKELLEN, Kt, CBE

ACTOR

Sir Ian was born on 25 May 1934. His first stage appearance was as Roper in A Man For All Seasons *and his films include* Scandal *and* The Shadow. *On television he has appeared in* David Copperfield *and* Othello *among others, and he has won a number of awards, including the Laurence Olivier Award.*

Ian McKellen

8 June 1994

dear Jonathan Gabay,

It's all very well to look for a meaning in your own life. But when such a meaning becomes institutionalised by any organisation, however well-intentioned, I get very nervous.

Yours ever

Ian McKellen

VIRGINIA McKENNA

FOUNDER OF ZOO CHECK CHARITABLE TRUST AND ACTRESS

Virginia was born on 7 June 1931 and was married to Bill Travers, who died in 1994. She currently runs the Born Free animal conservation fund. Her films include Born Free, Ring of Bright Water *and* An Elephant Called Slowly. *She has written a number of books including* Some of My Friends Have Tails *and* On Playing with Lions *(with Bill Travers).*

Live for each moment.

Give as much as you can and take as little as you need.

Live life with your eyes open - see the beauty of the world, and the suffering.

Live life with your heart open - let your compassion and love embrace all living things.

LORLE MICHAELES

AUSCHWITZ CONCENTRATION CAMP SURVIVOR

Lorle was born on 15 November 1912. She was interned with her brother, father and mother at Auschwitz Nazi death camp. Apart from her brother, her entire family were slaughtered through being gassed alive. She escaped from Germany to a new life in the United Kingdom. There she trained as a nurse and continued to care for patients until she was 62.

Dear Jonathan,

For 40 years, I had the privilege to work in children's hospitals, and appreciate the values of everyone's life, and now in my advance age of retirement, I still manage to enjoy some voluntary work, as well as my love for music, friends and children, and to me, these are the things that give 'meaning to life'.

Lorle Michaeles

PRESIDENT FRANÇOIS MITTERRAND

PRESIDENT OF FRANCE

François was born on 26 October 1916 and served in the French army between 1939 and 1940. He was taken prisoner and escaped back to France where he was active in POW and resistance movements. He later entered politics as Minister of Ex-Servicemen and became the Minister of State in 1947. In 1967 he became Minister of State for Justice, and in 1971 he was elected leader of the new Socialist Party. He was President of France from 1981 to 1995.

Je veux qu'à travers vous tous les jeunes couples parfois hésitants le sachent: la creation d'un foyer, oui, sans doute, c'est une aventure, mais tout est aventure dans la vie. Mais est-il ambition, accomplissement, epanouissement plus exaltants? Les enfants donnent un sens à la vie personnelle et un avenir au pays.

Je pense à ces derniers mots du grand savant Jacques Monod que chacun répéte en soi-même jusqu'à la fin: 'Je cherche a comprendre.'

I would like that via you, every young hesitant couple should know that the creation of the home is undoubtedly an adventure, but isn't everything in life an adventure? No ambition, accomplishment fulfilment could be more exhilarating than creating your home. The children give meaning to one as an individual and to the nation as a whole.

I recollect the last words of the greatly knowledgeable Jack Monod – words that each of us repeats to oneself to the end: 'I try to understand.'

THE RT HON. JAMES HENRY MOLYNAEUX, MP

POLITICIAN

James was born on 27 August 1920. He served in the RAF and has held several senior political posts. He is the leader of the Ulster Unionists and as such is one of the UK's leading spokespersons on Anglo-Irish political liaisons.

Dear Mr Gabay,

In your letter you ask, 'What is the meaning of life?'

My own humble view is that human beings, in the course of their life span, have a duty to add something to the well being of their planet and those who live thereon – the two objectives are inseparable.

There is now a greater awareness of that wider duty than there was in my school days and one hopes that awareness will steadily increase.

Yours sincerely,
James Molyneaux, MP

JOHN MONKS

GENERAL SECRETARY OF THE TRADE UNION CONGRESS

John was born on 5 August 1945 and joined the TUC in 1969. He was deputy general secretary of the TUC from 1987 to 1993. Apart from his duties as general secretary, he is also a trustee of the National Museum of Labour History.

Trades Union Congress

Congress House, Great Russell Street, London WC1B 3LS
Telephone: 071-636 4030; Fax: 071-636 0632; Telex: 268 328 TUCG

Your reference:

If replying please quote our reference:
S/JM/NM
When telephoning please ask for:

Date:
24 May 1994

Dear Mr Gabay

Thank you for your letter of May 23.

I am not sure that I can shed much light on your question - what is the meaning of life? I can only answer what is the meaning of <u>my</u> life.

In brief, I intend as General Secretary of the TUC to champion the interests of the underdog and to speak up for those who are not well placed to speak up for themselves.

In personal terms, courtesy, good humour and a strong sense of public duty are the qualities I most admire and to which I aspire to adhere.

Yours sincerely

JOHN MONKS
General Secretary

General Secretary: John Monks
Deputy General Secretary:
Brendan Barber
Assistant General Secretary:
David Lea, OBE

DESMOND MORRIS, DPhil

WRITER ON ANIMAL BEHAVIOUR AND TELEVISION PRESENTER

Desmond was born on 24 January 1928. He went to Birmingham University where he gained a BSc. His DPhil was awarded at Magdalen College, Oxford. He has dedicated much of his life to the study of animal behaviour. Desmond's TV work includes The Human Animal, The Animal Roadshow, The Animal Contract *and* Animal Country. *His publications include* The Biology of Art, The Human Zoo, Man Watching *and* The Human Animal.

From DESMOND MORRIS

30/7/94

Dear Jonathan Gabay,

      Thanks for your kind words about THE HUMAN ANIMAL. Yes, there will be a video set of the complete series before too long.

      Here is my quote.....

   LIFE IS A LITTLE TIME TO SPARE BETWEEN THE LIGHT OF BIRTH AND THE DARK OF DYING.

   LIFE IS THE TIME WHEN WE ARE LET LOOSE IN THE ADULT TOYSHOP OF THIS DELIGHTFUL PLANET.

   Best wishes.

STIRLING MOSS, OBE

CAR RACING CHAMPION AND COMPANY DIRECTOR

Stirling was born on 17 September 1929. He is the only Englishman to have won the Italian Mille Miglia (in 1955). He was twice voted Driver of the Year and competed in 494 races, rallies, sprints, land speed records and endurance runs (winning 222). He is now MD of Stirling Moss Ltd, director of Designs Unlimited Ltd and chairman or president of 30 motoring clubs.

Stirling Moss Limited

Jonathan Gaby Esq.,
32, Springfield Gardens,
LONDON NW9 0RS.   July 1st 1994

Dear Mr Gabay,

Hopefully the following will help:

"Life is to be lived, and hopefully in living, one can find pleasure, achievement, amusement, love, friendship and tranquility. To me, movement is tranquility."

Best regards and good luck,

STIRLING MOSS

46 SHEPHERD STREET LONDON W1Y 8JN   TELEPHONE: 071-499 7967 & 3272   FAX: 071-499 4104

Directors: STIRLING MOSS O.B.E., F.I.E.   V.K. PIRIE   S. PAINE   Registered Office: 35a HIGH STREET IVER BUCKS.   Reg. No. 542345

LADY PATRICIA MOUNTBATTEN OF BURMA, CBE, CD

CHARITY WORKER AND PATRON

Lady Mountbatten was born on 14 February 1924. She is one of the country's leading charity workers and has been a key figure with organisations such as the NSPCC, the Nurses Welfare Trust and the British Red Cross. She is patron of Kent Council on drug addiction and East Kent Hospice.

Dear Mr Gabay,

What is the meaning of life? If only there was an answer it would probably make life much easier! I have never given the question much thought myself, and I am not a religious person, but I suppose my philosophy has always been that the best and most useful way one can lead one's life is to try and be as helpful and caring as possible to all one's fellow human beings, wherever and whoever they may be.

I realise this is not really an answer to your question, but it does seem to me to give a meaning *to* life, and to supply a purpose and direction when needed.

If it were possible to answer your question there would really be no need to ask it!

With best wishes,
Yours sincerely,
Patricia Mountbatten of Burma

N

Life is like a game of cards. The hand that is dealt you represents determinism; the way you play it is free will.

JAWAHARIAL NEHRU

Life is one crisis after another.

RICHARD NIXON

The whole world is a narrow bridge and the fundamental principle is not to be afraid.

NACHMAN OF BRESLOV

RABBI JULIA NEUBERGER

FIRST FEMALE UK RABBI

Rabbi Neuberger was born on 27 February 1950. She was educated in London and is one of the country's most respected theological leaders. She has been a member of the BMA Ethics Committee, a member of INTERIM, an executive of UNICEF and a member of the Institute of Human Rights. Her books include Caring for the Dying Patients of Different Faiths *and* The Story of Judaism.

Dear Mr Gabay,

The meaning of life.

In one way, life, human life, has its own meaning. Jews value life itself above all else. You can ignore/transgress all mitzvot but three to save life (and one of those three is the prohibition against murder). So life – being alive – has its own meaning, and we are commended to do the best we can. But that is because it is God's creation – in whatever sense you like to take that – and we have to do everything we can to make the best of God's world, even when our own lives are going badly badly wrong. The meaning of life is to enhance God's plan for the world – though we have free will, we are instructed to preserve life, help others, make the world a better place. Trite though that seems, I think the nearest I can find to the meaning of life – which I would call the purpose of life – is the requirement to do what we can for everyone else, improving – and enjoying – God's creation.

Yours sincerely,
Julia Neuberger

DEREK NIMMO

ACTOR, AUTHOR AND PRODUCER

Derek was born on 19 September 1932. His first stage appearance was at the Hippodrome, Bolton, and his theatrical work has included Waltz of the Toreadors, Charlie Girl, Babes in the Wood *and* A Friend Indeed. *He has had several TV series including* All Gas and Gaiters, Life Begins at Forty *and* Just a Nimmo. *He has appeared in films such as* Casino Royal *and* The Amorous Prawn *and his books include* Derek Nimmo's Drinking Companion *and* As the Actress Said to the Bishop.

---

110 LEXHAM GARDENS
KENSINGTON
LONDON W8 6JE
Tel. No. 071-373 5236

12th May 1994

Dear Mr Gabay,

You ask me what the meaning of life might be. The truth is, I really have no idea. All I know is that, up to now, it has been tolerably good fun and I have enjoyed it a great deal.

I hope yours rapidly becomes jolly as well.

Yours ever,

DEREK NIMMO

O, P, Q

Life is an operation which is done in a forward direction. One lives towards *the future, because to live consists inexorably in* doing, *in each individual life* making *itself.*

JOSÉ ORTEGA Y GASSET

Man is only a reed, the weakest thing in nature; but he is a reed that thinks.

BLAISE PASCAL

When I was a young man, I had a passionate desire for the wisdom that is called Physical Science. I thought it a splendid thing to know the causes of everything; why a thing comes into being, and why it perishes, and why it exists . . . It seemed to me to be right that Mind should be the cause of all things, and I thought to myself, If this is so, then the Mind will order and arrange each thing in the best possible way.

PLATO

Life is only a short episode between two eternities of death, and even in this episode, conscious thought has lasted and will last only a moment. Thought is only a gleam in the midst of a long night. But it is this gleam which is everything.

HENRI PONCARÉ

Be wisely worldly, be not worldly wise.

FRANCIS QUARLES

REVD DR JOHN POLKINGHORNE

PRESIDENT OF QUEENS' COLLEGE, CAMBRIDGE

The Revd Polkinghorne was born on 16 October 1930. He was educated at Trinity College, Cambridge (BA, PhD, MA, ScD). He was ordained as a deacon in 1981 and a priest in 1982. He is currently president of Queens' College, Cambridge. His books include Models of High Energy Processes, The Way The World Is, Science and Creation *and* Reason and Reality.

Dear Mr Gabay,

I believe that this life alone would not make sense if death were to be its ending. In fact, I believe that a destiny awaits us beyond our death, in which the hope and courage and love we find in this world will have their true fulfilment. The meaning of life on earth is a preparation for that fuller life that awaits us in God's mercy. We are creatures whose destiny is to know the steadfast love our Creator has for us.

Best wishes,
Yours sincerely,
John Polkinghorne

SISTER HELEN PREJEAN

CHAIRPERSON OF THE NATIONAL COALITION TO ABOLISH THE DEATH PENALTY

Sister Helen was born in Louisiana, USA, on 21 April 1939. She is a member of the Sisters of St Joseph of Medaille. Her involvement with poor inner-city residents in New Orleans led to a prison ministry where she counselled death row inmates in the Louisiana State Penitentiary. She has accompanied men to the electric chair and witnessed their deaths. Her book, Dead Man Walking, *has been featured on media programmes on both sides of the Atlantic and is being made into a movie. She has been named as one of America's 100 Fearless Women.*

What is the meaning of life, I am asked, and from a unique perspective: what is the meaning of life as seen by death row inmates? I am asked to be their spokesperson because I am spiritual advisor to (some) death row inmates in Louisiana – five in all – which I have been doing for twelve years now, and I have accompanied three human beings to the electric chair and watched them 'ride the lightning' as tough tobacco-chewing 'Rednecks' like to say. I have watched three men be put to death before my eyes and I have watched them die a 1000 times before they sat in the dark oak chair.

'Ride the lightning', which is what we all do once born because of the way life is, flashing and sparking and over before we know it (can it be true? Am I fifty five years old?). Yes, we all 'ride the lightning' but to meet death from a death row cell after waiting five, eight, ten years – that is a unique perspective.

Death row is a confined life. You live in a 6 × 8½ ft cell 23 out of 24 hours a day. In the summer temperatures can get to 95°F. No cross ventilation. Sometimes you wet the sheet from your bunk in your lavatory and put the sheet on the cement floor and lie on it. There are two main emotions: boredom and fear. Boredom because each day is like every other day. Fear because the people all around you are serious about killing you. You walk a tightrope. Hopefully your lawyer (always a volunteer attorney in the appeals process) will find an issue in your case. A niche in the side of the bare-faced wall where you can get a footing. You walk the thin line between life and death. You get a date of execution six weeks away and your lawyers try to stop the train. Sometimes they do. Sometimes they don't. You know stories. Johnny Taylor, who walked right through because he had no attorney for his appeals. Robert Wayne

Williams walking to the electric chair and the phone rings in the death house. One of the courts wants to examine one more legal issue in the case. Williams is led back to his cell to await the verdict. One hour passes. The phone rings. No relief from the courts. He walks again to the chair. This time they strap him in and kill him.

Controlling the fear with the conscious mind is one thing, but sleep is another. During the last three days of his life, Pat Sannier tried not to sleep. He took cat naps. Because when he slept deeply he dreamed and in the dream the guards were coming to his cell to get him and he was screaming, 'No! No!' and they were dragging him and strapping him in the chair. Always the same dream. When conscious human beings are condemned to die, we die again and again in anticipation.

Of those I have accompanied to their death, all of them searched deep within their souls for a place of strength and calmness. Some called the source God. All prayed to be able to walk to their death with dignity. They begged God to hold their legs up. They didn't want to fail. They didn't want to show weakness before those who were killing them.

When I am with them in those last hours I always tell them of their value and their worth. I tell them that they are sons of God. I tell them that they are more than the worst thing they've ever done in their life.

And I have come away from the execution chamber set on fire for life and justice. I spend most of the energies of my life educating people about the death penalty and why we must abolish it. I know that I am one of the few witnesses who can tell people what really goes on.

FAY PRESTO

MAGICIAN

Fay Presto began his career as a motorcycle messenger and in sales. Now a 'she', Fay is arguably one of the country's most talented magicians. She has cast her magical spells for the likes of Elton John, Eric Clapton, Rod Stewart, Dustin Hoffman, Michael Caine, HRH The Princess of Wales and many others. Fay has appeared on numerous TV shows including Wogan *and* Trick *on* 2 *and was the subject of a special 40-minute documentary. During 1995, Fay will appear in her own TV show for Sky Television.*

C/o Jenny Dunster,Leisure Services Agency,439-445 Godstone Road Whyteleaf Surrey CR3 OYG

Dear Jonathan

Thank you for taking the trouble to write, I have been completely overwhelmed by the depth of support that people have shown. There have been so many letters, some brief, some long, all charming. Answering them has become a monumental task, but each one is so important, each is a gesture of hope, a real encouragement. Out there, I now know are so many wonderful people that one cannot help but be inspired.
There have been over two hundred letters to me, five hundred to points of view and dozens of phone calls. Not one negative comment, not one, and not one enquiry from the programme makers! The silence from Television land has been deafening, but the whisper from the mail bag is unrelenting. I HAVE to give it another shot!

At this stage it is only the letters, the wonderful, touching, supportive, encouraging letters that are keeping me going and maintaining my sanity. None of the rest of it makes any kind of sense. . If I do get through this it will be in no small part because of the kind words 700 total strangers took the trouble to write.

It really would be wonderful to tour a show, to have an audience come to find me would be so nice but the vast majority of my work is still corporate and/or private. I have taken the liberty of putting your address on a mailing list. Systems permitting, if a show ever does happen, a faint hope but a hope; you will get to hear.
Thank you, you have provided a real tonic, just when I needed it most. The meaning of life? Answers on the back of a post card follows!

Fay Presto!

Now this I can't believe, I mean I'm sitting here with 60 or 70 fan letters demanding answers to urgent but more reasonable questions, and I'm pondering the meaning of life for some Mr. Joe Public to put in a book!! Being a 'Celebrity' is not all polar bear skin rugs and chocolates! And emergence from a nervous breakdown is no excuse, there's been a few of us there.

I'm not a good person to ask, the cosmos played a pretty horrid practical joke when it gave me an inside that didn't match the outside! Dealing with that used up most of the spare capacity for philosophical maundering.

Survive without quitting early, and try to leave the place a little better than you found it. A better world starts here. It starts with you, it starts with me and it starts now!

Any system of belief or philosophy that brings comfort is to be cherished, the point at which they bring discomfort should be challenged.

Fay Presto!

JONATHAN PRYCE

ACTOR

Jonathan was born on 1 June 1947. He has been in many successful films and stage plays, including Hamlet, Miss Saigon *and* Oliver! *(theatre) and* Something Wicked This Way Comes, Brazil *and* A Business Affair *(films). Television work includes* Roger Doesn't Live Here Anymore *and* Selling Hitler.

JONATHAN PRYCE

Living
In
Fearful
Expectation ! JP

R

As I grow to understand life less and less, I learn to live it more and more.

JULES RENARD

There is no wealth but life.

JOHN RUSKIN

Real life is, to most men, a long second best, a perpetual compromise between the ideal and the possible.

BERTRAND RUSSELL

BERYL REID, OBE

ACTRESS

Beryl was born on 17 June 1920 and her first stage appearance was in Bridlington in 1936. She was first seen on the London stage in 1951. As one of England's best-loved actresses she often appears on television and radio. Beryl received Best TV Actress Award (BAFTA) in 1983 for Smiley's People. *Her books include* So Much Love *(autobiography) and* Beryl, Food and Friends.

BERYL REID O.B.E.

May 30 1994

Dear Jonathan

Thank you for your letter. My theory is — when you wake up in the morning —

a)   Be glad that you are alive

b)   Enjoy each day as much as you possibly can.

c)   Get pleasure from all the small things that you see. An animal, a flower, a tree, and at the end of the day you will find that however you feel you will have enjoyed the day to the best of your ability.

With best wishes *+ good wishes*

Beryl Reid

GORDON RICHARDS

RACE HORSE TRAINER

Gordon was born on 7 September 1930. He became an apprentice jockey in 1943 and a National Hunt jockey in 1950. In 1964 he became a trainer for the National Hunt. To date he has trained two Grand National winners – Lucius (1978) and Hello Dandy (1984) – and more than a hundred winners in a season.

Dear Mr Gabay,

The meaning of life, is the good you have done and the love you have given. The only things you can take with you when you go.

Gordon Richards

S

*To use Heidegger's expression, the world outside of that – NOTHING –
this NOTHING is human reality itself as the radical negation by means of
which the world is revealed . . . Human reality is that which causes there
to be nothing outside of being.*

JEAN-PAUL SARTRE

*The meaning of life is the road, not the goal. For each answer is delusive,
each fulfilment melts away between our fingers, and the goal is no longer a
goal once it is attained.*

ARTHUR SCHNITZLER

Life is short but sweet.

SOPHOCLES

*Life is as tedious as a twice-told tale. Vexing the dull ear of a drowsy
man.*

WILLIAM SHAKESPEARE

*Life is a flame that is always burning itself out: but it catches fire again
every time a child is born.*

GEORGE BERNARD SHAW

Fear God, keep his commandments, for this is the purpose of man.

KING SOLOMON

ALEXEI SAYLE

COMIC ACTOR AND WRITER

Alexei was born in Liverpool on 7 August 1952 and was educated at Southport and Chelsea Schools of Art. His films include Gorky Park *and* Supergrass *and on television he has starred in* The Young Ones, Alexei Sayle's Stuff *and* Didn't You Kill My Brother? *His writing work includes* The Young Ones, The House of the Ford Cortina *and* Comic Roots.

ALEXEI SAYLE

Dear Johnathan,

I do not know what life means, but I do know what eichhörnchen means – it's German for squirrel.

VICTOR SPINETTI

ACTOR

Victor was born on 3 September 1933. He began his career in 1953 in a concert party in Wales and went on to appear in revues in London. He continued to appear in various films such as The Beatles' classic, Help!, *and plays such as* Oh What a Lovely War! *(for which he received a Tony Award). He was also involved with various foreign productions of* Hair *and* Jesus Christ Superstar.

Dear Jonathan,

The point of this pen on this paper, before this is typed, is all I need to know at this moment.

From moment to moment until we stop, meanwhile be as loving and understanding to the people who are close to you.

Voltaire said 'Make your garden grow' or as Blake said, 'See heaven in a wild flower and eternity in a grain of salt' or as I say,

HELL

Is what we make of our lives.

HEAVEN

Is how alive we can be.

Victor Spinetti

ROY STENTAFORD

DUSTMAN

Roy was born in 1936. He was a dustman for over a decade and is now a waste management HGV driver. He is married with grown-up children.

> To me the meaning of life is to
> live my life as I want to, as best
> as possible
> To love my wife and children
> To love my grandchildren
> To have as many laughs as possible
> To make people laugh with me if possible
> To get on with life, as best as possible
> And in the end, I like to think
> that I have meant something in
> life to someone?

JAMES STEWART

HOMELESS PERSON

James was born in 1932. He is homeless. I met him in Leicester Square, London, where he was selling The Big Issue *magazine (a publication whose proceeds go towards helping the homeless).*

The meaning of life is to live in comfortable surroundings, to love one another, not to criticise people who are down on their luck or disabled or coloured. We are all human beings. To help where you can . . . and live with people no matter what their position in life, to help others and not be ashamed of receiving help, to be religious no matter what creed . . . and try to aspire to better things than a cardboard box or a doorway with the proper help, which is not always forthcoming. We could all live a meaningful life.

SIR PETER STRAWSON, Kt

PROFESSOR OF METAPHYSICAL PHILOSOPHY

Sir Peter was born on 23 November 1919. His various books on philosophy include Introduction to Logical Theory *and* Freedom and Resentment. *He is a fellow of Magdalen College, Oxford.*

Dear Mr Gabay,

To your question 'What is the meaning of life?' I doubt if I can offer any answer which will be of use to you – partly because the meaning of the question itself is to me unclear.

If asked for the meaning of a text, quotation or saying, I know I am being asked for an interpretation or translation or exegesis.

If asked for the meaning of a natural phenomenon, I may be being asked either (a) how it came about (the genesis); or (b) what its likely consequences will be. Asked about the phenomenon of life in general, (a) had better be addressed to the natural sciences; and (b) is probably unanswerable. If asked specifically about human life, then (a) is a question for evolutionary biologists, and (b) is again unanswerable.

It may be that the question is intended to be about the *purpose* or the *value* of human life. In neither case does a general answer seem to be possible. Purposes and values vary from individual to individual and from society to society. Cosmic purpose? Divine purpose? I see no sense in the idea of the former and no reason to believe in the latter.

Of course the case is different with individuals at times. As Keats wrote, of a little animal he saw scurrying along: 'The creature has a purpose and his eyes are bright with it.'

Yours sincerely,
Peter Strawson

DAVID SUCHET

ACTOR

David was born on 2 May 1946. He was educated at Wellington School and named the Best Drama Student of 1968 in LAMDA. One of his most famous roles on TV has been as Agatha Christie's Hercule Poirot, which he has played since the late 1980s. His films include Harry and the Hendersons *and* Thirteen at Dinner.

David Suchet

June 8, 1994

Dear Jonathan,

Thank you for your kind letter.

The meaning of life for me is :

'To learn to love those I don't like. To respect, have compassion for, show kindness and generosity to all those I would normally turn away from.'

My desire is that God grants me strength to abide by these guidelines.

I hope this is helpful.

With best wishes

ABRAHAM BEN YOSEF SUISSA

ISRAELI SOLDIER

Abraham is a sergeant in the Intelligence unit of the Israeli army. His mother is a locally renowned spiritual medium. His family was one of the founding settlers in a new town on the outskirts of the Negev desert in Israel.

As an Israeli soldier (three years' compulsory service and subsequent years doing reserve duty), my meaning of life is not a struggle for personal survival but more to help achieve peace so that my children will not need to go to war.

In battle I also give a lot of thought to the enemy facing me. He too has a wife and children and he too cares for them and wants to save his family from the tragic consequences of war.

I pray that our next generation will pave a new meaning of life unbeknown in the Middle East region for nearly half a century, a life of sincere comradeship enjoying neighbourly peace and happiness.

T

The meaningless absurdity of life is the only incontestable knowledge accessible to man.

COUNT LEO TOLSTOY

When we remember that we are all mad, the mysteries disappear and life stands explained.

MARK TWAIN

Oh isn't life a terrible thing – thank God.

DYLAN THOMAS

As we get older, we realise that we all get our priorities wrong. Everyone today seems to worry more about wealth and not their health as we did years ago. Also people had more warmth and respect for their fellow beings.

HARRY TIANO – TAXI DRIVER

THE RT HON. LORD NORMAN TEBBIT

POLITICIAN

Norman Tebbit was born in 1931 in Enfield and became a journalist at the age of sixteen. After National Service in the RAF he became an airline pilot. He was elected to parliament in 1970 and was made Employment Secretary in 1981 and Trade and Industry Secretary in 1983. He and his wife Margaret both sustained injuries in the 1984 IRA bombing in Brighton.

Right Honourable **LORD TEBBIT CH**

House of Lords
LONDON SW1A 0PW

John F Gray Esq
British Red Cross
National Headquarters
9 Grosvenor Crescent
LONDON SW1X 7EJ

4 October 1994

Dear Mr Gray

Thank you for your letter informing me of Mr Jonathan Gabay's project.

My only contribution might be:

'If life has a meaning it is by design obscured from mortals'.

Yours sincerely

123

MOTHER THERESA OF CALCUTTA

NOBEL PEACE PRIZE WINNER

Mother Theresa was born in former Yugoslavia in 1910. She went to India in 1928, where she joined the Sisters of Loretto (an Irish order in India) and taught at a convent school in Calcutta, taking her final vows in 1937. In 1948, Mother Theresa left the convent to work in slums. She went to Paris for medical training before opening her first school for destitute children in Calcutta. In 1971 she was awarded the Pope John XXIII peace prize. She was awarded the Nobel Prize for Peace in 1979.

+LDM

MISSIONARIES OF CHARITY
54A. A. J. C. Bose Road,
Calcutta - 700016. India

Dear Jonathan Gabay,

Thank you for your kind letter. I am sorry for the delay in replying, since I was out and have only just returned to Calcutta.

Life is the most beautiful gift of God to mankind. Each one of us no matter how great or small have been created in the image of God, for greater things — to love and to be loved. Let us keep this joy of loving each other through sharing with all.

God bless you.

lee Teresa mc

RIGHT REVD BERNARD THOROGOOD, OBE

FORMER GENERAL SECRETARY OF THE UNITED REFORMED CHURCH

Revd Thorogood was born on 21 July 1927. He was educated at Glasgow University (where he received an MA) and the Scottish Congregational College. He was ordained in 1952 in the Congregational Church and then followed a 'calling' to become a missionary in the South Pacific Islands. From there he became general secretary for the Council for World Mission. His books include Guide to the Book of Amos *and* Our Father's House.

Dear Mr Gabay,

We, and all living things, are part of the creative process. We do not see either the beginning or the end of the process, but we know that small slice of it which contains the story of humanity.

We are all actors on that stage and everyone has a part to play. I believe that behind the creative process there is the mind and power of God the Creator, who wills the process into being and will complete it at the end.

Each life has meaning as part of the whole story. We are each given life so that we may further the purpose of God, to create harmony, to develop each talent and personality, to express the love of Christ and to help overcome all the pains of the creative process.

For there is no creation without pain. In our lives we all meet sorrow at parting, sickness, inequality of resources, fear of death. Our calling is to strive for these elements to become creative, not destructive, to take away the bitterness with the sweetness of God's hope in us.

The great symbol of God's creative love is, for me, the resurrection of Christ. Life from the tomb. We are given that renewing power so that out of all the dark places of human experience we may rise again. Despair is the enemy.

Just as the Creator never despairs of us, so we can have hope in one another even through disappointment or disagreement. We are all loved by God, who has no favourites. There are no outsiders.

So the meaning of life, or its essential character, is for each person to play a part on the mighty stage of God's creative purpose. The story began with chaos and is to end with God's reign of love, peace and celebration. Our lives are to be a positive part of that long journey.

I hope that is helpful.

Yours sincerely,
Bernard Thorogood

ALEXANDER THYNN

SEVENTH MARQUESS OF BATH

Alexander was born on 6 May 1932 and educated at Eton College and Christ Church, Oxford, where he received a BA and an MA. He is the director of Cheddar Caves and Longleat Enterprises and is an author and composer. His home, Longleat House, is one of England's most visited cultural landmarks, famous for its architecture as well as its wildlife park. He has a permanent exhibition of murals (painted between 1964 and 1969) in private apartments at Longleat House.

We find ourselves in existence, not from any act of choice which we ourselves made, but from the choice of parents with whom we may (or may not) build up satisfactory bonds of relationship. In some cases they instil us with their own sense of purpose in life: an inspiration to continue with some particular problem-solving quest, to the attainment of specific goals, which may involve a replication of their own achievements, or the fulfilment of a prowess which was desired (but was deficient) within their own life's performance. On the other hand we may find ourselves creating our own sense of purpose in life, from ideas which derive entirely from our own experience.

No matter which the approach however, the notion of a purpose in life stands central to any lasting sense of involvement with this universe in which we all dwell for the span of years that we find to be our lot. Provided that we achieve some degree of success in the implementation of this sense of purpose, it contributes greatly towards both our self-esteem and our peace of mind; and a final point to note is that a society in which self-esteem and peace of mind can be widely promoted within the individuals that it contains, furnishes us with the best possible formula for the attainment of the general happiness.

I am suggesting that these are the levers we need to watch when assessing our individual ability to align ourselves with the dictates of this universe. The universe is a gentle master so long as we can find the way of tending to its needs within the realisation of our own personalised identity; but it promptly emerges in the guise of an ogre, if we establish our own interests on a level too much aside from, or above, those of the common lot.

It also displays random tantrums, which may well destroy the lives (or just the wellbeing) of individuals deserving of a better fate. And the random strike of death or misfortune on a tranquil day must be anticipated as part of the pattern, into which the history of each and every one of us has been woven. Naturally we hope for better things, but we must be ready to shield ourselves from dismay if disaster should befall.

It is after all best that we should live in acceptance of the idea that our experience is contained within a strictly finite life, upon a planet whose history is finite, within a universe which is itself finite – despite the fact that it stands there in permanence and in perpetuity. There can be little purpose in fretting concerning what our individual lot may turn out to be, provided that we are currently doing all within our power to fulfil the sense of purpose on this earth, to which we may have committed ourselves.

We find ourselves with a perceived number of problems on our plate. We tackle these problems within the spirit of a problem-solving quest, in an awareness that the solutions we adopt will unleash problems of a different kind. Our concern should never be to withdraw from this quest, but to be careful instead to ensure that the problems on our plate are decreased, rather than augmented, by the solutions that we engender.

Each individual's problem-solving question is a highly personalised affair. There are no generalised rules on offer. But the creation of one's special niche within society (indeed within the universe at large) involves a variety of routine practises which most people take for granted. But each individual needs to establish what will be the nature of the family form, from which he will be making his attack upon life's fortune. He will need to be clear as to the nature of the political groupings, whose ideals may be sufficiently similar to his own, to warrant a joint approach in the quest for such solutions. He must also be clear on the identity and nature of the state, which will permit such political groups to operate with the necessary degree of freedom to have some possibility of attaining their goals; and he must know what legitimate assistance and encouragement he can expect to receive from the services of this state.

Regardless of any assistance that the individual might anticipate will be coming his way, it is far wiser that he should realise that throughout his existence, he should be capable of standing on his own feet in the pursuit of the goals that he has freely chosen for himself. And it is usual that he would have selected for himself a territorial base, or home nest, from which to operate. The concept of a home is important in that it stands as the point of connection between the individual and the universe. Without it, he is found rootless and at a disadvantage; but from inside it, he confronts the rest of the world as if from behind a shield.

We find ourselves in this world without either requesting or arranging that we should be here. But we are liable to accept the fact, because suicide represents too negative (and irreversible) a solution. The identification of a purpose in life may be largely a survival technique, but it is also the key to human happiness. Quite apart from the statement of such a generalised approach to the problems of living, the bulk of the work has to be left to the individual, in discovering where his special talents for involvement might lie. That is precisely what makes the humanity in us to start smouldering, hopefully to ignite as something more inspirational than a wet squib, so that our thoughts and aspirations may finally explode in a brilliance of radiation throughout mankind.

BILL TIDY

FREELANCE CARTOONIST, WRITER, PLAYWRIGHT, TELEVISION AND RADIO
PRESENTER

Bill was born on 9 October 1933. He began work as a layout artist for an advertising agency but his unique cartoon style coupled with a witty writing style made him an outstanding cartoonist and writer in his own right. TV work has included Tidy Up Walsall *and* My City. *Radio broadcasting includes* The News Quiz *and* I'm Sorry I Haven't a Clue. *His many publications (written and illustrated) include* Sporting Chances, Laugh with Bill Tidy, Up the Red Up the Blues *and* The World's Worst Golf Club.

DAME CATHERINE TIZZARD, GCMG, DBE

GOVERNOR GENERAL OF NEW ZEALAND

Dame Catherine was born on 4 April 1931. She was educated at Matamata college and Auckland University. Prior to being elected as Mayor of Auckland, she was a teacher of zoology. She became Governor General of New Zealand in 1990.

Dear Mr Gabay,

Dame Catherine has told me that in order to answer your question she can do no better than quote Aldous Huxley. Towards the end of his life he said:

'It's a bit embarrassing to have concerned all one's life with "the human problem" and find at the end, that one has no more to offer by way of advice than "try to be a little kinder".'

Yours sincerely,
Hugo Judd
Official secretary

MOST REVD DESMOND TUTU, LTh, MTh

SOUTH AFRICAN ECCLESIASTIC

Revd Tutu was born on 7 October 1931. He was educated at the University of South Africa, and King's College, London, where he studied theology. He became an Anglican parish priest in 1960, the first black bishop of Johannesburg in 1984 and archbishop of Cape Town in 1986. A fierce critic of the apartheid system, his awards include Martin Luther King Jr Peace Award, the Third World Prize and the Nobel Peace Prize.

Life is for living, for loving. We wilt if we don't love, for we are made for belonging, for community, since to be human is possible only through relationship, as a person is a person through other persons. Community is life – a gentle, caring community, sharing and compassionate, where people count not because of status, achievement, race, culture or whatever else, but because they are made in God's image to be creative, affirming, sustaining, to be the best they have it in them to be.

U, V, W

By knowing God one is released from all fetters.
SHVETASHVATARA UPANISHDAD

Life is the childhood of our immortality.
JOHANN WOLFGANG VON GOETHE

I have maintained from first to last that the laws of Economics are the laws of life.
PHILIP H. WICKSTEAD

Life is an unanswered question, but let's still believe in the dignity and importance of the question.
TENNESSEE WILLIAMS

It is the essence of life that it exists for its own sake.
A. N. WHITEHEAD

JOHN WALL

CHAIRMAN, ROYAL NATIONAL INSTITUTE FOR THE BLIND AND SECRETARY
GENERAL OF THE EUROPEAN BLIND UNION

John was born on 4 June 1930. He has been totally blind since he was eight years old. After taking a law degree at Oxford he qualified as a solicitor. He was the first blind person to be appointed to judicial office and is the UK's only blind judge.

Put the question, 'What is the meaning of life?' to a lawyer and he is likely to reply: 'On average nine years.' This information about the length of his sentence is no doubt crucial to a convicted murderer and those members of his family who were not his victims but in the context of this essay it can be judged flippant.

Little better is the lawyer's other reaction – to reach for the dictionary. Admittedly the Concise Oxford Dictionary gives twenty-one meanings for the world 'life' – one might think this to be 'un embarras de richesses'. But to give a dictionary meaning could reasonably be characterised as an evasion.

On a more serious level, the question involves the necessary implication that life has a meaning. One way of dealing with the issue would be simply to say that life has no meaning. That seems to me to be an eminently arguable hypothesis, but I do not intend to adopt it.

The second definition of 'life' in the Concise Oxford Dictionary is 'the period between birth and death'. In accepting that definition I find myself plunging into deep water. I was fortunate enough to have a happy and secure childhood with parents who both loved me dearly and also instilled in me certain moral values. They would have liked to have instilled certain religious beliefs as well. They belonged to what was then called the Conservative Evangelical Wing of the Church of England and I was a regular churchgoer until I 'flew the nest'.

Which brings me to a confession of beliefs or more accurately disbeliefs.

1) I do not believe in reincarnation. This makes me feel a killjoy. It would be great fun to find that in a previous life I had been a Roman Centurion or a Medieval Master Singer – but reincarnation just seems to me to be a fairy tale.

2) I do not believe in the signs of the Zodiac. Are star signs a joke? Perhaps they are although I am told they have a scientific basis. I never cease to be surprised at the number of people who take them very seriously. Again I am a killjoy, though I must confess that I am a

Gemini (perhaps I should say we are Gemini) and I get a lot of fun reading my horoscope in the popular press.

3) I do not believe in an afterlife. Adopting this position makes me feel very guilty. How many bereaved people have been partly consoled by thinking that their loved one who has died is actually living in a better place? How dare I tell them that they are deluded? I am saying that one of the fundamental beliefs of Christianity and Islam is wrong. I accept that this is arrogant but I feel I must be honest. Afterlife is inherently improbable and there just does not seem to be any evidence to support its existence.

4) Is there a personal God? Here I suppose I vacillate between atheism (saying 'no') and agnosticism (saying 'don't know'). Religious people always take the view that if you are not with them, you are against them. I respect that stance and, as I cannot say that I believe in God, I cannot subscribe to Christianity or Islam or Judaism. Again, I have to accept the arrogance in my position and I again plead that I am only trying to be honest.

None of what I have said so far is particularly original or particularly clever or particularly profound. But I had to get it out of the way before I could address the question: 'What is the meaning of life?' The creator (and I don't see why the creator must be a personal God) gives us certain attributes by heredity and we gain others from the environment we grow up in. Receiving these attributes seems to be a matter of chance and how we develop as human beings is certainly a matter of chance. Nature (the impersonal creator) shakes the box containing the dice and it is pure luck whether we end up dying young or old, achieving success or failure, being happy or miserable, and so on.

What are we meant to do? No human being is self contained or self sufficient. We are all members of a community. We interact with our fellows. We form relationships such as parent and child, husband and wife or 'just' friendship.

If life is to have any meaning we must make the best of our talents. The rest of humanity owes us no more than we owe them. 'Do as you would be done by' (is it from Kingsley's *Water Babies*?) rings in my ears from my early childhood. The world does not owe us a living. But other human beings must treat us as equals. We must lay down rules of conduct, not just for the rest of the world but for ourselves. If we seek privileges – beneficial rules which apply only to us – we shall not deserve to succeed.

So we should aim to achieve as much freedom for the individual as possible but that freedom and the right to it must be exercised responsibly. Beware of the seven deadly sins. Try to practise the four cardinal virtues.

MARJORIE WALLACE

JOURNALIST, AUTHOR, PLAYWRIGHT, BROADCASTER, CHIEF EXECUTIVE OF SANE

Marjorie studied philosophy at University College, London, and has worked for ITV and the BBC. In 1972 she was one of the team who exposed the thalidomide tragedy. HRH The Princess of Wales said of her work: 'There are shining examples of what can be done, such as a series of articles by Marjorie Wallace which not only laid the foundation of contemporary understanding of schizophrenia but also led directly to the foundation of SANE.'

Since diagnosed with cancer a year ago I've been even more diligent in looking for the meaning of life, only hoping it will emerge before it is too late. But the more effort the search, the more elusive the solution. Death, of course, is the ultimate comment on personal existence, yet its shifty, watery image is as unreliable as it is empty.

As a very young child I would speak, then write gloomy poems which grappled with these cosmological questions. One poem, in particular, was about a tree which stayed awake all night so that it could witness the goblins and evil spirits. It learned too much. Its lonely search for the truth of the night displeased the spirits, who left it stripped of its bark and leaves, its blossoms torn, while all the other trees of the orchard who failed to keep vigil, greeted the dawn pretty and unharmed.

Perhaps I should have learned my lesson then: that it is both uncomfortable and dangerous to be too aware. But I didn't. I went on to study philosophy and psychology and became an investigative reporter for *The Sunday Times*.

There I discovered that I could articulate the sufferings of other people: give through words, shape, colour and symmetry to the wastelands of human misery. What broke my heart was how relentless and random were the tragedies I described: a mother turning her brain-damaged child every hour of every night; thalidomide people trapped in their limbless bodies; victims of dioxin, asbestos, road accidents or negligence. By turning their ordinary stories into dramas – even campaigns – some at least could be given new zest and purpose.

Those with schizophrenia or serious mental illness presented a special challenge and one with which I could most easily identify. A sufferer, John, once said to me: 'Once your mind has touched the edges of the universe, you are never the same again.' He reminded me of my tree: the tormented night vigils experienced by so many mentally ill people, the fragility of their world, their exposure to every threat. Too many voices. Too many shadows. And for their families, especially the mothers, wearied by days and nights of watching terror invade the minds of their children, there seemed no source of comfort. It was *their* sadness and courage that drove me to leave my career in journalism and help form the mental health charity, SANE.

As for myself, I feel less and less comfort in the poems and words I used to cherish. Individual existence seems of little value and any meaning must lie in the continuum. All we can do is to paint our dreams on the patch of worn canvas allotted to us. We must use the brightest freshest colours we can find, knowing that the shapes will blur, the colours wash away and that soon someone else will come to paint over our brief effort at creation.

JULIE WALTERS

ACTRESS

Julie was born on 22 February 1950. Her first big acting break came in 1980 with Educating Rita. *Two years later she played the role of Rita in the film version of the play for which she won the Variety Club Award for Best Film Actress and a BAFTA award. Her films include* She'll Be Wearing Pink Pyjamas, Personal Services *and* Buster. *Her television work includes* Wood and Walters, Victoria Wood as Seen on TV, The Secret Diary of Adrian Mole *and* GBH.

Julie Walters

Dear Jonathan Gabsay ~
I think life is a series
of lessons that are there
to enhance the evolution of
the spirit. ~ Now there's deep.
Sincerely,
Julie Walters

ZOË WANAMAKER

ACTRESS

Zoë kindly agreed to submit her contribution to the book only a few months after her father Sam sadly died. Her stage work includes A Midsummer Night's Dream, Guys and Dolls, A Comedy of Errors *and* The Time of Your Life. *She has appeared on television in* Sally for Keeps, The Devil's Crown, Poor Little Rich Girl, Prime Suspect *and* Love Hurts.

ZOË WANAMAKER

C/o Conway Van Gelder Ltd
18-21 Jermyn Street
London
SW1Y 6HP

24th June 1994

Dear Jonathan Gabay

You have twisted my arm and I have come up with this:-

The meaning of life is improving on what came before, which is impossible.

Yours sincerely

Zoe Wanamaker

SIR HAROLD WILSON, KG, OBE, FRS

FORMER BRITISH PRIME MINISTER AND FIRST LORD OF THE TREASURY

Lord Wilson was born on 11 March 1916. Before entering national political life he was a lecturer in economics, and a fellow of University College, Oxford. He became an MP in 1945 and was then appointed Parliamentary Secretary to the Ministry of Works. In 1947 he became Secretary for Overseas Trade and President of the Board of Trade. He became Prime Minister in 1964 and was made a life peer in 1983. He died peacefully in his sleep at St Thomas's Hospital, London, on 24 May 1995 at the age of 79.

I am particularly proud and honoured that Lord Wilson agreed to provide this contribution. It was one of the few times that he agreed to have his words published during a prolonged period of illness.

Dear Mr Gabay,

I am afraid it is quite impossible to respond to your request in a few sentences.

For me, however, the answer must lie in the teachings of Christ.

With good wishes,
Yours sincerely,
Harold Wilson

PAUL WOOD

CARTOONIST

Paul is one of the country's most original cartoonists. He is a regular contributor to Punch *and other leading national publications. He agreed to send his contribution even though a close member of his family was seriously ill.*

PATRICK WRIGHT

ILLUSTRATIVE CARTOONIST

Patrick was born in 1945 in North Wales. He had no formal training as an illustrator but came from a family of illustrators. He started to work on children's comics in 1972. Since then his work has been seen in the Evening Standard, *on advertising material and in various other publications such as* Punch. *His published work includes bestselling books such as* 101 Uses for a John Major *and* 101 Further Uses for a John Major. *He is currently working on an illustrative biography of John Major.*

Courtesy of Chris Beetles Ltd, St James's, London

141

X, Y, Z

I am moved to pity when I think of the brevity of human life.

XERXES

Be wise today; 'tis madness to differ.

EDWARD YOUNG

When I think of all the books I have read, and of the wise words I have heard spoken, and of the anxiety I have given to parents and grandparents, and of the hopes that I have had, all life weighed in the scales of my own life seems to me preparation for something that never happens.

WILLIAM B. YEATS

In the beginning they established life and non-life, that at last the worst existence should be for the wicked, but for the righteous one the Best Mind.

ZARATHUSTRA

To be happy, to become creative, man must always be strengthened by faith in the meaning of his own existence.

STEFAN ZWEIG

FRED ZINNEMANN

FILM DIRECTOR

Fred was born on 29 April 1907. He studied law at the University of Vienna before becoming an assistant cameraman in Paris and Berlin. In 1929 he emigrated to the US and headed for Hollywood where he eventually became an assistant to various directors. In 1948 he was given the opportunity to direct his own film. His many subsequent films include From Here to Eternity, Oklahoma!, The Day of the Jackal *and* Five Days One Summer. *His autobiography,* A Life in the Movies, *was published in 1992.*

Dear Mr Gabay,

In reply to the question contained in your round robin letter I can only say that the meaning is to realise that we are *not* by accident in this world, and to act upon this fact.

Sincerely, and with good wishes,
Fred Zinnemann

AFTERWORD

So, do you now know what the meaning of life is? Or does the search continue?

I have found it fascinating and intriguing as well as reassuring and touching to refer to this book time and time again. For me it's more than just a collection of answers from people whom I respect. It is a unique snapshot in time, taken just a few years before a new millennium. It shows a broad cross-section of people from all walks of life who share their otherwise private thoughts.

When things go wrong, people often ask, 'What is it all about?' To ask, 'What is the meaning and through it, the purpose of life?' is even more appropriate when things go *right*.

Perhaps, ultimately, as you hold this book, you have the answer.

It is in your hands. each time you close this book of life, re-open your own. Live it and discover the truth.

J. Jonathan Gabay